POCKET

ALGARVE

TOP SIGHTS • LOCAL EXPERIENCES

CATHERINE LE NEVEZ

Contents

Plan Your Trip

Tavira (p56)

Explore Algarve 33

Worth a Trip

Survival Guide 145

Special Features

Welcome to the Algarve

Soaring cliffs, hidden sea caves, golden beaches, scalloped bays and sandy islands lure visitors to Portugal's Algarve region. Surrounded by the Atlantic, the coast is a water-sports paradise, while the hilly hinterland has historic castle towns, whitewashed villages, rolling countryside covered in almond trees and citrus orchards, rural farmhouse restaurants and glorious hiking.

Carvoeiro (p89)
SOPOTNICKI/SHUTTERSTOCK ©

Top Sights

Cacela Velha

Picturesque coastal Portuguese village. p70

STEFANO_VALERI/SHUTTERSTOCK ©

IRINASEN/GETTY IMAGES ©

Surfing the West Coast

Protected landscapes and pounding surf. p136

MAURO RODRIGUES/SHUTTERSTOCK ©

Faro's Sé

Climb the cathedral's bell tower. p36

TONY MILLS/SHUTTERSTOCK ©

Parque Natural da Ria Formosa

Lagoons, barrier islands and beaches. p38

On the Water in Lagos

Water sports and cruises galore. **p106**

LORIEL/SHUTTERSTOCK ©

FRANCISCOJORGAN/SHUTTERSTOCK ©

Via Algarviana

Hike the hilly Algarve hinterland. **p96**

Fortaleza de Sagres

Mighty clifftop fortress. **p122**

Cabo de São Vicente

The continent's most southwesterly point. **p124**

Beaches

The coast of the Algarve is a seemingly endless series of beaches. The climate and atmosphere feel Mediterranean, but this is the Atlantic, so good waves and first-rate water sports are available alongside more sedate family-oriented paddling zones. With more than 150 beaches, this is one of Europe's capitals of sun, sand and surf.

Options Galore

There are so many superb beaches in the Algarve that any attempt to list the best is, in a sense, doomed to failure. You're sure to find your own favourite that doesn't feature here. One of the region's appealing features is that there's such a variety of conditions in a relatively small area.

West Coast Beaches

The west coast is particularly good for surfing, with a series of west- and southwest-facing beaches that see some big swells. They are divided by sharp schist headlands that provide some excellent point breaks when conditions are right.

South Coast Beaches

The south coast in general has softer waves, with a series of picturesque beaches backed by sculptured limestone formations in the western half of the region. The eastern segment has a series of evocative island beaches that are the outer section of the complex of dunes and lagoons that forms the Parque Natural da Ria Formosa. Accessed by boat, they are romantic spots.

Best Remote Beaches

Praia de Vale Figueira Lonely, lovely stretch of sea spray and sand at the end of a long byroad. (p139)

Ilha da Armona Part of the Parque Natural da Ria Formosa, this island has remote, deserted sands and a busier family-oriented strip. (p38)

Ilha de Tavira Large sandy island with an excellent beach opposite Tavira,

SERGIO STAKHNYK/SHUTTERSTOCK ©

and long, quiet strands to explore. (p64)

Best Family Beaches

Praia de Odeceixe Has a kid-friendly river side and barrelling ocean breakers. (p143)

Praia Fluvial Not to be outdone by the coast, this inland town has created a tiny beach resort on a quiet river bend. (p61)

Praia do Martinhal This postcard-pretty Sagres beach is calm and shallow. (p127)

Praia do Carvoeiro Carvoeiro's central beach is small, friendly and patrolled by lifeguards in summer. (p89)

Best Surf Beaches

Praia da Arrifana Classic surf beach with a beach break and a point break. (p143)

Praia da Bordeira This Carrapateira beach (and its twin Praia do Amado) has great surf and coastal scenery. (p137)

Praia da Amoreira Backed by wild, rolling dunes, this spectacular river-mouth beach has left- and right-handed breaks. (Pictured; p137)

Praia do Monte Clérigo Exposed in all directions, Monte Clérigo's famed left-handed break is reliable virtually all year. (p139)

Praia de Odeceixe Shifting sandbanks, consistent swells and a surf school see Odeceixe's beach attract pods of surfers. (p143)

Best Strollable Beaches

Praia da Falésia Take a 6km stroll along this scenic beach fringed by variegated ochre and white cliffs. (p76)

Praia da Marinha Sculpted limestone makes this one of the region's most scenic beaches for strolling. (p89)

Meia Praia Stroll 4km along gorgeous Meia Praia from the party town of Lagos. (p116)

Praia da Galé The 5km-long Praia da Galé is a prime place to escape nearby Albufeira's crowds. (p76)

Eating

Seafood reigns: octopus, prawns and fish, including prized sardines, all star on Algarvian menus. The signature dish is a cataplana (seafood stew slow-cooked in a large copper vessel resembling a metal clam). You'll also find traditional Portuguese grilled meats and poultry, and localised specialities like Monchique's blood sausages.

Best Traditional Dining

A Casínha Savour traditional Portuguese dishes at this smart Sagres spot. (p131)

Faz Gostos In Faro's old town; presents sophisticated dishes and outstanding wines. (p47)

Pont'a Pé Reliably excellent family-run place serving great fish to hungry surfers. (p143)

Best Innovative Dining

Vila Joya Near Albufeira; often regarded as Portugal's best fine-dining restaurant. (p79)

O Tonel Cutting-edge Portuguese cuisine and dining room to match in Tavira. (p67)

Vila Adentro Sophisticated twists on Portuguese classics in a romantic, old town setting. (p46)

Best Dining with Views

O Luar da Fóia Just outside Monchique; an excellent rustic restaurant with a view. (p102)

A Fábrica do Costa Seafood restaurant in a stunning setting right on the water near Cacela Velha. (p71)

Recanto dos Mouros Views from the terrace of this farmhouse restaurant take in Silves' castle. (p90)

Best Vegetarian Dining

Mó Veggie Bistro Organic vegetarian and vegan dishes in Aljezur. (p141)

Gengibre e Canela Sociable all-vegetarian restaurant with a daily buffet in the centre of Faro. (p48)

Mum's A postsurf favourite in Sagres with great retro decor. (p131)

Best Cafes

Kiosk Agapito Brilliant beach bar/cafe above Praia de Odeceixe's surf using local ingredients in ingenious combinations. (p141)

Pastelaria Rosa Historic tiled cafe in Silves with lots of enchantment. (p89)

Pastelaria Tavirense The social heart of Tavira. (p59)

Mimar Café Excellent all-round choice in Lagos. (p115)

Best Rural Dining

Jardim das Oliveiras Wonderfully rustic local secret in the hills behind Monchique, with tables beneath the trees. (p101)

Monte da Eira Country restaurant offering high-class food in a converted mill. (p83)

Veneza A charming rural restaurant worth seeking out near Albufeira. (p79)

Hidden Alvor Dining

Descend 33 shallow steps, then take a lift through the sandstone and walk through an underground tunnel to reach hidden bar-restaurant **Caniço** (☎282 458 503; www.canicorestaurante.com; Aldeamento Prainha 5, Alvor; ⏲10am-4am Mar-Nov; 📶), which opens onto a little beach wedged between soaring cliffs. Barbecued fish is the speciality of its restaurant, along with classic *cataplanas* (seafood stew; pictured). Sangria, punches, cocktails and champagne are highlights of the drinks list. DJs spin nightly, when dancing takes place on the sand and the cliffs are illuminated with neon lights.

Activities

Activities in the Algarve aren't limited to the water. Inland, the Via Algarviana traverses the region and there are plenty of other hiking trails. Other land-based pursuits include horse riding and rock climbing.

Walking

The website www.walkalgarve.com is an excellent resource for hikers, with details of long and short walks throughout the region, including route information, GPS coordinates, topographical profiles and seasonal considerations, as well as detailed maps.

Cycling & Mountain Biking

The 214km-long Ecovia do Litoral cycling trail (www.ecoviadolitoralalgarve.com) links Cabo de São Vicente with Vila Real de Santo António.

Hilly terrain in the Algarve's interior makes it ideal for *bicicleta todo terreno* (BTT; mountain biking), with several operators offering trips, bike hire and advice.

Rock Climbing

The Algarve's rocky coast and interior are tailor-made for rock climbing. Contact Algarve Adventure (p140), which runs trips (gear and transport included).

Horse Riding

Horse riding is a fantastic way to experience the Algarve's countryside. Riding centres throughout the region offer lessons, treks and pony rides for kids.

Best Walking

Via Algarviana This long-distance walk crosses the region; some of its stages make great day walks. (p96)

Rota Vicentina Tramp down the Algarve's west coast. (Pictured; p140)

Percurso dos Sete Vales Suspensos Spectacular clifftop walk between glorious beaches. (p89)

Rocha da Pena Scale this 479m-high limestone rock in the Serra do Caldeirão region. (p83)

VITALY FEDOTOV/SHUTTERSTOCK ©

Fóia It's a lovely hike from Monchique up to the Algarve's highest point. (p99)

Walkin'Sagres Great walking excursions around Sagres. (p127)

Burros e Artes Multiday treks across the Algarve with donkeys carrying the gear. (p140)

Best Horse Riding

Albufeira Riding Centre Wide range of horse rides for all abilities; well-cared-for horses. (p78)

Tiffany's Horse-riding excursions near Lagos. (p113)

Country Riding Centre Horse rides for all levels in the Silves countryside. (p89)

Best Mountain Biking

Mountain Bike Adventure Full range of excursions, from gentle downhills to technical black routes. (p113)

Alternativtour Mountain-biking tours and more. (p101)

Outdoor Tours Good biking (and walking) excursions. (p113)

Be Climate Ready

- Temperatures in the Algarve can be scorching in high summer; check forecasts via IPMA (www.ipma.pt). Wear a hat, use sunscreen and carry plenty of water.

- Forest fires regularly affect inland areas such as Monchique during summer. Heed warnings and fire bans; Portugal News (www.theportugalnews.com) has the latest news in English.

For Families

It's hard to envisage a destination that is better set up for kids than the Algarve, so it's a deservedly popular family-holiday spot. Apart from the great weather and the dozens of child-friendly beaches, there's a plethora of family activities on offer, from zoos and water parks to boat trips, horse riding and more.

Algarve Advantages

One of the big advantages of the Algarve as a family destination is the short travel times between attractions, minimising the risk of kids getting frazzled by long car trips. Children are very welcome just about everywhere, and lots of restaurants have a children's menu.

Forward Planning

Though the region is chock-full of family attractions, a bit of pre-planning is rewarding. There are many water parks, but children under five aren't allowed on most rides, so if you've got a range of ages, it might be wise to choose a park that has alternative attractions such as animals. Queues for rides can be long in July and August, but visiting midweek can help. Food and beverages are expensive, and while bringing your own is often technically not permitted, checks are rare.

Family Accommodation

Accommodation is easy, with numerous apartments offering kitchen facilities and flexible sleeping arrangements. Even in hotels and B&Bs, most choices will put a cot or extra bed into a room for a small extra charge. Read the fine print though, as there are increasing numbers of boutique or resort-style hotels that don't accept younger children.

Best Water Parks

Slide & Splash Portugal's best water park will keep kids and adults entertained for hours. (p88)

GLYNSIMAGES2013/SHUTTERSTOCK ©

Aquashow A massive complex with water-park attractions, roller coasters and an on-site hotel. (p77)

Aqualand The huge loop-the-loop slide has the biggest wow factor. (Pictured; p77)

Krazy World Water park and crocodiles, appropriately separated. (p78)

Parque Zoológico de Lagos Popular zoo west of Lagos. (p112)

Burros e Artes Donkey treks suitable for younger children. (p140)

Albufeira Riding Centre Recommended horse-riding set-up; good with kids of all ages. (p78)

Best Family Activities

Mar Ilimitado Kids love spotting dolphins on trips run by this Sagres operator. (p127)

Lands Older kids can try sea kayaking in the calm waters off Faro. (p45)

Algarve Surf School Offers parallel lessons for kids, so the whole family can learn at the same time. (p143)

Tops Tips for Parents

Save time and money by prepurchasing tickets for big-ticket attractions (eg water parks) online.

- Car-hire companies can usually provide child seats; book in advance as numbers are limited.
- Discreet breast-feeding in public is normally fine.
- Formula (including organic brands) and disposable nappies (diapers) are widely available at pharmacies and supermarkets.

Water Activities

JOSERPIZARRO/SHUTTERSTOCK ©

For such a coastal destination, it's no surprise that what you can do on or under the water is basically only limited by the time you have available. There are numerous operators offering boat trips of all types, or take to the ocean yourself with a surfboard, scuba tank, sea kayak or kite rig.

Best Boat Trips & Wildlife Watching

Mar Ilimitado Environmentally focused dolphin- and birdwatching trips out of Sagres. (p127)

Formosamar Excellent wildlife-spotting boat trips around the Ria Formosa park. (p45)

Natura Algarve Dolphin- and bird-spotting trips around the eastern Algarve. (p46)

Passeios Ria Formosa Various boat trips to explore estuaries and islands. (p66)

Best Diving

Divers Cove Multilingual centre offering hire, dives and accredited courses. (www.divers-cove.com; Quinta do Paraíso; 1-day discovery course €135, 1 dive with/without gear €50/35, 6 dives €250/175)

Blue Ocean Reliable centre with a full offering of courses, dives and hire. (p115)

DiversCape Based at the harbour in Sagres; competent, recommended diving operator. (p128)

Best Kayaking

Lands Reliable set-up offering kayak hire and tours; based in Faro. (p45)

Dolphins Driven Coastal explorations from Albufeira. (p76)

Taruga Tours Hires kayaks to paddle into the astonishing Benagil Caves. (p89)

Best Surfing & Kitesurfing

Arrifana Surf School A complete range of hire and lessons. (p137)

Algarve Surf School Based at Praia do Amado, with transfers from other towns. (p143)

Odeceixe Surf School Friendly set-up based at Praia de Odeceixe. (p143)

Lagos Surf Center Surf classes with family options available. (p115)

Sagres Natura Sagres-based surf school. (p127)

Kitesurf Eolis Excellent kiting east of Tavira. (p66)

Algarve Water Sport Kitesurfing, windsurfing and board riding, with transport from Lagos. (p115)

Birdwatching

TONY MILLS/SHUTTERSTOCK ©

The Algarve is an increasingly popular destination for birdwatching. Its geographical position makes it an important stopover for migratory birds, while the quantity of wetland environments offers an ideal habitat for waders and ducks. Offshore are numerous species of seabirds, including several that are rare in the rest of Europe.

Sagres Portugal's southwest corner is good year-round for seabird watching and particularly noteworthy during the autumn migration season, as hundreds of raptors pass overhead towards Africa.

Reserva Natural do Sapal de Castro Marim (p61) Important winter visitors at this 20-sq-km stretch of marshland and salt pans bordering the Rio Guadiana include greater flamingos, spoonbills and Caspian terns. In spring it's busy with white storks.

Parque Natural da Ria Formosa (p38) This coastal park of tidal estuaries and dune islands attracts over 20,000 wintering birds. Iconic species include the purple gallinule and hard-to-spot little bittern.

Lagoa dos Salgados Between the resorts of Albufeira and Armação de Pêra, this shallow marshy lagoon is a popular place to watch waders, including flamingos, spoonbills (pictured) and the purple gallinule, and a large number and variety of duck species.

Birdwatching Resources

Algarve Tourism (www.visitalgarve.pt) produces a regional birdwatching guide.

Birds and Nature (☎913 299 990; www.birds.pt; half-/full day from €100/160) runs various Algarve tours.

Simon Wates (☎282 639 418; www.algarvebirdman.com) is a recommended birdwatching guide.

Festivals

MAURO RODRIGUES/SHUTTERSTOCK ©

Feira de Santa Iria (www.cm-faro.pt; ⏲Oct) Faro's biggest traditional event honours St Irene with fairground rides, stalls and entertainment. It takes place over nine days in the second half of October in a large parking area, the Largo de São Francisco, on the eastern side of the old town.

Carnaval de Loulé (www.cm-loule.pt; ⏲Feb or Mar) Just before Lent, Loulé celebrates Carnaval (pictured) over three days. Exuberant festivities include parades with tractor-drawn floats, live music and a grand ball. Friday is the children's parade and Sunday's the big one.

Festa da Ria Formosa (www.cm-faro.pt; ⏲late Jul-early Aug) This 11-day-long event held at the height of summer is one for seafood-lovers. Fishers and others set up stalls and prepare their wares, from crustaceans to other ocean delights, at the Largo de São Francisco. Concerts add to the fun atmosphere.

Nossa Senhora da Piedade (⏲Mar or Apr) Linked to ancient maternity rites, Loulé's *romaria* (religious festival) is the Algarve's most important. On Easter Sunday a 16th-century image of Our Lady of Pity (or Piety) is carried down from its hilltop chapel, 2km west of town, to the parish church. Two weeks later, a procession of devotees lines the steep route to the chapel to witness its return.

Feira dos Enchidos Tradicionais (www.cm-monchique.pt; ⏲early Mar) Monchique's traditional sausage festival takes place during the first weekend in March in the main square. You'll also catch performances by folklore troupes and find handicrafts for sale.

Festival Med (www.festivalmed.pt; ⏲late Jun) Loulé's three-day world-music festival has gained a reputation as a quality event and now attracts strong line-ups of international performers, as well as dance, handicrafts exhibitions and street theatre.

Feira Medieva (www.cm-silves.pt; ⏲mid-Aug) Silves' Medieval Fair takes place over 10 days in August at venues around town. Period costumes, dances, jesters, feasts, traditional food and handicrafts all evoke life in the 11th to 13th centuries.

FolkFaro (www.folkfaro.com; ⏲mid-Aug) Faro's big folk festival features lots of dance (with local and international folk groups), live music and street fests over eight days at various venues around town.

Festival da Sardinha (www.festivaldasardinha.pt; ⏲Aug) Portimão's sardine festival is a five-day celebration of Portugal's favourite fish, accompanied by associated music, dance and festivities. It's held at the old fishing quarter, the Zona Ribeirinha de Portimão.

Nightlife

MAURO RODRIGUES/SHUTTERSTOCK ©

Abundant nightlife all along the coast draws a mainly foreign clientele. Lagos is the epicentre for the party crowd; Faro and Albufeira also have lively after-dark scenes. Local Sagres and Super Bock beer, wine (from the Algarve and around Portugal) and liqueurs (such as fig or carob) are all popular and bars are plentiful.

Best Local Drinking Spots

Nana's Bar In Praia da Rocha; has a far more local scene than the waterfront venues. (p93)

Barlefante Tucked away in a narrow alley, this is Monchique's after-dark hideaway. (p103)

Taberna dos Frades There's a great local vibe in this welcoming Loulé bar. (p80)

Ref A Tavira stalwart with retro decor, contemporary music and great atmosphere. (p69)

Best Scenic Drinking Spots

O Castelo Marvellous views over the water from Faro's old town. (Pictured; p49)

Kiosk Agapito Fabulous Odeceixe beach cafe with great drinks, music and locally sourced food. (p141)

Best Postsurf Drinking Spots

O Sargo Right by the sand in Aljezur with regular live music and full-moon parties. (p143)

Agua Salgada One of the liveliest of a strip of surfer-oriented cafe-restaurant-bars in Sagres. (p133)

The Garden Laid-back Lagos beer garden with a barbecue and resident cat. (p117)

Bahia Beach Bar Essential hang-out on Meia Praia. (p117)

Best Cocktails

Bon Vivant One of Lagos' best all-round choices, with a roof terrace, upbeat bar staff and excellent cocktails. (p117)

Columbus Bar Faro's best cocktail bar mixes superlative drinks and has a stunning vaulted interior, as well as grab-'em-if-you-can outdoor tables. (p50)

Tavira Lounge By the river in Tavira; seamlessly converts itself from a cafe by day to a cocktail lounge-bar by night. (p69)

Dromedário Twists on cocktails at this lively Sagres bar include watermelon-and-ginger martinis. (p133)

Markets

AMNAT30/SHUTTERSTOCK ©

Portugal is still a country where markets are an important part of commerce and play a big role in society. The Algarve has plenty of interesting ones to visit. Marvelling at the fresh fish in the municipal food markets is always a delight, while rotating village markets combine cheap tat with authentic locally produced items.

Municipal Markets

In many ways the best and most authentic markets are the municipal covered markets found in most towns. These open Monday to Saturday mornings and are great for a stroll to examine the fresh fruit and vegetables, and fish and meat counters. It's the best option for self-caterers, and the most sustainable way to shop for food in the Algarve. In fishing towns, the *lota* is where the fresh fish off the boats is auctioned to restaurants and fishmongers; not a place to make purchases yourself, but often an interesting spectacle.

Other Algarve Markets

Other markets occur weekly, fortnightly or monthly on different days. These tend to combine local specialities – warm woollens, brassware and Moorish-influenced ceramics, for example –with low-quality sweatshop-produced underwear and other cut-price clothing. Still, they are always worth a wander, and you can find some good bargains. Some of them have second-hand stalls, too.

Loulé Local produce and delicacies inside a landmark 1908 revivalist neo-Moorish building. (p81)

Olhão Housed in 200-year-old brick buildings on the waterfront, with seafood stalls and cafes. (p53)

Lagos Seafood is a speciality at Lagos' covered market. (p119)

Faro Modern covered market with on-site restaurants. (p50)

Historic Architecture

SAIKO3P/SHUTTERSTOCK ©

Best Cathedrals & Churches

Igreja de São Lourenço de Matos The blue-and-white-tiled interior of this small roadside church makes it one of the most stunning sights in the Algarve. (p75)

Sé, Faro The centrepiece of Faro's old town offers a museum and super views from its bell tower. (p36)

Igreja de Nossa Senhora do Carmo This Faro church is most notable for its spooky chapel built of skulls and bones. (Pictured; p43)

Igreja de Santo António Accessed through the municipal museum in Lagos, this is a baroque extravaganza. (p112)

Nossa Senhora da Conceição This chapel in Loulé has an undistinguished exterior, but a vibrant baroque interior. (p75)

Igreja Matriz, Monchique Hill-town church with several typically offbeat Manueline architectural features. (p99)

Sé, Silves The best-preserved Gothic church in the Algarve has a high, simple and typically elegant interior. (p87)

Museu de Arte Sacra Superbly restored 18th-century chapel in Albufeira with a collection of religious art from the surrounding region. (p76)

Best Castles & Fortresses

Fortaleza de Sagres Stern bastions guard an open expanse of clifftop with extensive coastal views. (p122)

Castelo, Silves The restored walls of this Moorish-era castle offer commanding vistas over this atmospheric town. (p87)

Castelo, Castro Marim The Algarve's most impressive medieval fortress offers unforgettable views into Spain. (p61)

Castelo, Tavira The shell of the walls of this formerly formidable castle house a peaceful botanic garden. (p59)

Castelo, Alcoutim Overlooking the Guadiana in the northeast Algarve, this atmospheric castle contains a museum. (p61)

Castelo, Aljezur Top of the town in this popular base for surfers, this fortress is bare but atmospheric. (p140)

Fortaleza da Ponta da Bandeira As fortresses go, this is shoe-box sized, but makes an interesting visit on the Lagos waterfront. (p109)

Cathedral Etiquette

It is considered disrespectful to visit churches as a tourist during Mass. Taking photos at such a time is definitely inappropriate.

Museums

AMNAT30/SHUTTERSTOCK ©

Museu de Portimão This brilliant former tuna cannery gives all the details about the industry and more. (Pictured; p93)

Museu Municipal, Aljezur Interesting displays on ethnography and the Moorish era, plus access to other museums around town. (p141)

Pólo Museológico de Salir Small display in what's left of Salir's castle. (p83)

Museu do Mar e da Terra da Carrapateira Atop the surf village of Carrapateira is an excellent display on maritime and local life. (p139)

Museu Municipal, Faro One of the Algarve's best archaeological museums, with high-quality pieces from different periods housed in a beautiful building. (p43)

Museu Municipal, Lagos An astonishingly varied collection, this museum will have something for everyone. (p112)

Museu Municipal, Loulé Occupying the town's castle; has an interesting and wide-ranging display. (p76)

Farol de São Vicente Small but perfectly formed, this little museum at the end of Portugal covers navigation and lighthouses. (p125)

Museu Municipal de Arqueologia This museum in Silves includes a fabulous in-situ Moorish well and parts of the town walls. (p88)

Núcleo Islâmico Tavira's most interesting museum focuses on the town's Islamic past. (p63)

Ways to Save

- Most of the Algarve's museums are small: good to bear in mind when budgeting your time.
- A student card will get you reduced admission to almost all sights. Those aged over 65 with proof of age will save cash.

Golf

AMA/SHUTTERSTOCK ©

With benevolent weather and over 50 courses in a relatively small area, the Algarve is one of Europe's top golfing destinations. High-end courses with big-name designers and state-of-the-art landscaping predominate, though there are also some humbler, cheaper options.

Monte Rei (☎281 950 960; www.monte-rei.com; Sitio do Pocinho Sesmarias, Vila Nova de Cacela; green fees €218; ⏰8am-6pm) Overlooking the Serra do Caldeirão mountains, Portugal's top-rated golf course, par 72 Monte Rei was created by golfing legend Jack Nicklaus. It's 15km northeast of Tavira.

Dom Pedro (☎289 310 333; www.dompedrogolf.com; Volta do Medronheiro, Vilamoura; green fees from €155) In the sprawling resort of Vilamoura, 15km southwest of Loulé, Dom Pedro has five high-standard golf courses, including the par 72 Victoria course, which has hosted the Portugal Masters every year since 2007.

Penina Golf Resort (☎282 420 200; www.penina.com; N125, Penina; green fees €127) Situated 7.5km northwest of Portimão, the Algarve's original golf resort's par 73 Sir Henry Cotton championship course was built in 1966.

San Lorenzo (☎289 396 522; www.sanlorenzogolfcourse.com; Quinta do Lobo; green fees €190) Past the airport, 19km west of Faro, this par 72 course borders the Ria Formosa.

Vale de Milho (☎282 358 502; www.valedemilhogolf.com; Rua de Vale de Milho; green fees €16; ⏰8am-sunset) Ideal for beginners and families, this friendly nine-hole course is 2.7km east of Carvoeiro.

Golf Resources

- Club hire is available at Faro Airport; book your set at www.clubstohire.com.
- The website www.algarvegolf.net offers discounted green-fee reservation at many of the Algarve's courses.
- Hotel group Pestana (www.pestanagolf.com) runs several of the Algarve's more affordable courses.

Four Perfect Days

Day 1

TONY MILLS/SHUTTERSTOCK ©

The **Faro** region has a fabulous variety of attractions that showcase the history and natural environment of the Algarve. Start in Faro's *cidade velha* (old town), climbing the bell tower of the **cathedral** (p36), and stop by the **Igreja de Nossa Senhora do Carmo** (p43) and its skull-and-bone chapel.

Take an afternoon boat trip to appreciate the intriguing landscapes and waterscapes of the **Parque Natural da Ria Formosa** (p38).

Station yourself at **O Castelo** (p49) for a sunset drink, then choose from one of Faro's excellent dining options, such as exquisitely tiled **Vila Adentro** (p46) or bargain-priced student favourite **A Venda** (p48).

Above: Purple swamp hen, Parque Natural da Ria Formosa (p38)

Day 2

SOPOTNICKI/SHUTTERSTOCK ©

The Algarve's refreshingly undeveloped far west has superb surf beaches and maritime history. Head first for the **Fortaleza de Sagres** (p122), then the spectacular cliffs at **Cabo de São Vicente** (pictured; p124).

In the afternoon wind your way up the coast. Stunning scenery stretches between Carrapateira's beaches **Praia da Bordeira** (p137) and **Praia do Amado** (p137). Also check out **Praia de Vale Figueira** (p139) and **Praia da Amoreira** (p137).

In pretty **Aljezur**, enjoy sunset views at the **castelo** (p140) or over a seafood feast at panoramic restaurant **O Paulo** (p142). Finish with drinks and live music in summer at **O Sargo** (p143).

CHRISTOPHE CAPPELLI/SHUTTERSTOCK ©

Head to hill village **Monchique**. Hike (or drive) to the top of the Algarve's highest peak, **Fóia** (p99), then soak in Caldas de Monchique's **spa** (p101), before lunch at enchanting rural restaurant **Jardim das Oliveiras** (p101).

Drive to postcard-pretty **Silves** with its Moorish **castelo** (pictured; p87), Gothic **cathedral** (p87) and intriguing well in its **Museu Municipal** (p88).

Descend to buzzing **Lagos** for superb dining: try sandside **Bar Quim** (p114) or stylish **Atlântico** (p114). Lagos' varied nightlife is the Algarve's best, spanning rooftop cocktails at **Bon Vivant** (p117) to beers in laid-back, al fresco **The Garden** (p117), along with wine bars, dive bars, rock bars and nightclubs.

JUAMPITER/GETTY IMAGES ©

Begin in the picturesque **Serra do Caldeirão**. Visit the delightful wooden toy factory **Fábrica de Brinquedos** (p83) near Alte and Salir's little **museum** (p83), before travelling to the coast via the beautiful tiled church **São Lourenço de Matos** (p75).

Stroll the riverside in **Tavira** (pictured), explore the old town and visit the absorbing **Nucleo Islâmico museum** (p63), then drive out to charming coastal village **Cacela Velha** (p71) to catch the evening light.

Back in Tavira, dine on grilled fish at down-to-earth **Casa Simão** (p67) or cutting-edge contemporary Portuguese cuisine at **O Tonel** (p67), ending with a cocktail at **Tavira Lounge** (p69).

Need to Know

For detailed information, see Survival Guide p145

Language

Portuguese; English widely spoken.

Currency

Euro (€)

Visas

EU citizens can stay indefinitely. Many other nationals can enter for up to 90 days; from 2021, ETIAS preauthorisation is required.

Money

ATMs are widespread. Most accommodation providers and upper-end restaurants accept credit cards.

Mobile Phones

EU phones don't incur roaming charges. Cheap local SIM cards for unlocked phones are readily available.

Tipping

Around 10% in restaurants (15% in pricier places) and bars with table service. Round up taxi fares to the nearest euro.

Daily Budget

Budget: Less than €80

Dorm bed: €15–€25

Simple guesthouse or hotel: €50–€60

Self-catering, or *prato do dia* (daily special) in a cheap restaurant: €8–€12

Bottle of local beer (33cL): €1.50

Train ticket from Faro to Lagos: €7.30

Midrange: €80–€150

Double room in a midrange hotel: €60–€130

Two-course evening meal: €20–€30

Carafe of local wine: €6–€8

Surfing lesson including board and wetsuit hire: €60

Top End: More than €150

High-end double hotel room: from €130

Three-course evening meal in top restaurant: €40–€70

Advance Planning

Several months before If you're coming in the peak summer months of July or August, reserve your accommodation and car hire now – the earlier, the better.

One month before Make reservations for high-end and/or popular restaurants, tee times at upmarket golf courses and prepurchase water-park tickets.

One week before Book your kitesurfing lessons, cruises or other water-based activities.

Arriving in the Algarve

Faro Airport

Faro Airport is just 7km west of the town centre.

Próximo (www.proximo.pt) city buses 14 and 16 run to the bus station (€2.20, 15 minutes, two per hour), an easy stroll to the centre.

The trip into town by taxi costs around €20, plus €2 or so for each item of luggage. The fare is 20% higher after 10pm and on weekends.

Faro Train Station

Faro's train station is 500m north-west of the centre.

Albufeira (€3.35, 30 minutes, every two hours)

Lagos (€7.30, 1¾ hours, every two hours)

Lisbon (€22.90, four hours, five daily)

Olhão (€1.45, 10 minutes)

Porto (€42.40, six to eight hours, four daily)

Getting Around

Bus

The bus network connecting towns along the Algarve coast and to Loulé is good, but services heading inland are more limited.

Car

You can pick up a hire car in most main towns, equipped with an electronic toll tag to cater for the Algarve's road tolls.

Train

Trains (www.cp.pt) connect Faro and Vila Real de Santo António, and Faro and Lagos (and Loulé).

Algarve Regions

West Coast Beaches (p135)
The west coast has utterly spectacular and gloriously unspoilt surf beaches and welcoming small towns.

Monchique & Around (p95)
An appealing hill town, Monchique straddles the long-distance Via Algarviana and has some great day hikes and a lovely spa village.

Via Algarviana

Cabo de São Vicente

Sagres & Around (p121)
On a promontory at the end of Portugal, Sagres is a laid-back surf town offering great coastal scenery and maritime history.

Lagos (p105)
Much more than a party town, postcard-perfect Lagos offers top beaches, a handsome historic centre and excellent restaurants.

Silves & Around (p85)
This former Moorish stronghold with a castle, cathedral and museum is one of the Algarve's most picturesque towns.

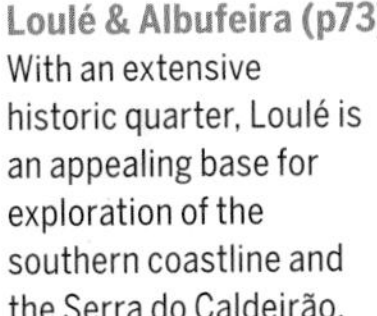

Loulé & Albufeira (p73)
With an extensive historic quarter, Loulé is an appealing base for exploration of the southern coastline and the Serra do Caldeirão.

Faro & Around (p35)
The region's capital has a charming waterside old town, excellent boat trips, and a lively restaurant and bar scene.

Tavira & Around (p57)
Set around a river, this pretty town is eminently strollable. Explore unspoilt island beaches and the gorgeous village of Cacela Velha.

Explore The Algarve

Worth a Trip

Walking Tours

Driving Tours

Kayaking in Lagos (p106) JUAMPITER/GETTY IMAGES ©

Explore

Faro & Around

The Algarve's capital has a more distinctly Portuguese feel than most of the region's resort towns, with an attractive marina, pretty parks and plazas, and a picturesque cidade velha (old town) ringed by medieval walls containing winding, cobbled pedestrian streets, squares, museums, churches and al fresco cafes. On Faro's doorstep are the lagoons of the Parque Natural da Ria Formosa, beaches and sandy islands.

The Short List

- ***Faro's Sé (p36)*** *Climbing the tower of the cathedral crowning Faro's old town.*
- ***Parque Natural da Ria Formosa (p38)*** *Exploring this intricate system of lagoons and islands stretching for 60km along the coast.*
- ***Igreja de Nossa Senhora do Carmo & Capela dos Ossos (p43)*** *Getting goosebumps in the bone chapel at Faro's baroque church.*
- ***Museu Municipal (p43)*** *Discovering art and archaeological treasures at Faro's municipal museum.*
- ***Milreu Ruins (p51)*** *Time-travelling back to Roman days at the extensive ruins outside the charming village of Estói.*

Getting There & Around

Faro Airport is the region's international gateway.

Buses serve destinations across the Algarve.

Trains from Faro's train station connect to coastal Algarve destinations.

Faro Map on p42

Street in Faro ANIAD/SHUTTERSTOCK ©

Top Sight

Faro's Sé

The centrepiece of the Cidade Velha, the sé was completed in 1251 but heavily damaged in the 1755 earthquake. What you see now is a variety of Renaissance, Gothic and baroque features. Climb the tower for lovely views across the walled town and estuary islands.

MAP P42, C5

www.paroquiasedefaro.org

Largo da Sé

adult/child €3/free

10am-6pm Mon-Fri, 10am-1pm Sat Jun-Sep, 10am-5.30pm Mon-Fri, 10am-1pm Sat Oct-May

Bell Tower

The cathedral's bell tower has panoramic views over old Faro and beyond to the marina and bay, and the estuary and islands of the Parque Natural da Ria Formosa. You needn't fear for your thigh muscles though: it's only 68 steps to the top and there's a rest stop halfway. Apart from the orange trees, landmarks on the square below include the 18th-century Paço Episcopal; it's the successor to the previous bishops' dwelling trashed by British troops in 1596.

Church

The church's interior clearly shows the variety of architectural styles that have been applied here: vaulted Gothic chapels stand to either side of the altar (pictured) and Renaissance arches divide the naves. Most of the rest is baroque, with some elaborate altarpieces in the side chapels, and a striking German-built 18th-century organ.

Museu Capitular

The cathedral museum houses an assortment of chalices and monstrances, as well as priestly vestments. There are some fine painted wooden statues that once had pride of place in altarpieces, but were superseded. More alarming is the reliquary collection, housing physical remains of various saints, including both forearms of St Boniface.

Garden

Formerly the cathedral cemetery, the garden is now notable for two small chapels. One, dating from the 17th century, is dedicated to the archangel São Miguel (St Michael). The other is a small 18th-century shrine built of bones: this type of construction was popular at the time and was designed as a reminder of the transitory nature of earthly life.

★ Top Tips

- There's a telescope at the top of the bell tower, but make sure you have a €0.50 coin if you want to use it.
- Counterpoint a visit to the historic cathedral with a stop at contemporary art gallery Galeria Trem (p44) just 80m south.

Take a Break

For a light meal or a drink with views, O Castelo (p49) is a good bet.

With a pretty terrace in the heart of the old town, Vila Adentro (p46) offers some modern takes on classic Algarve dishes.

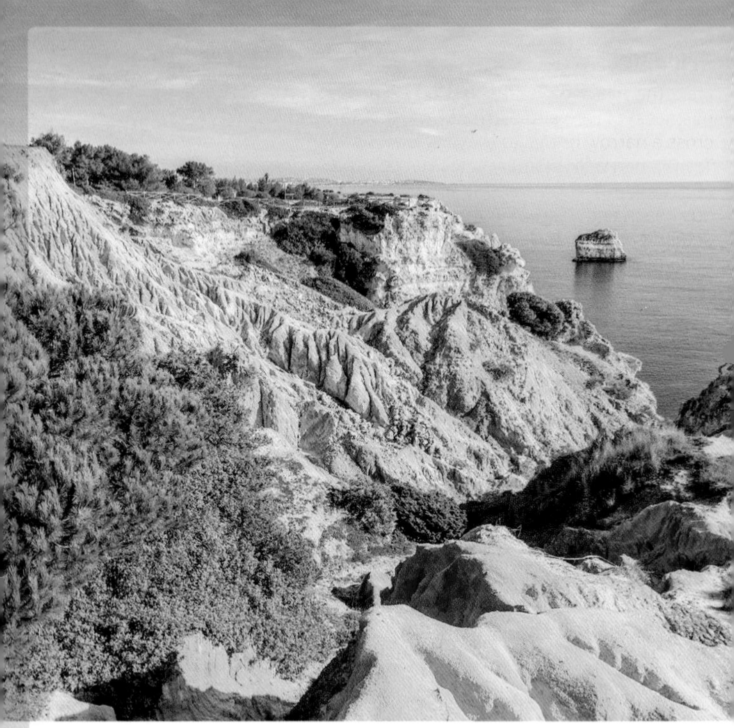

Top Sight

Parque Natural da Ria Formosa

Encompassing 18,000 hectares, this sizeable system of lagoons and islands stretches for 60km along the Algarve coastline from west of Faro to Cacela Velha. It encloses a vast area of sapal *(marsh),* salinas *(salt pans), creeks and dune islands. The marshes are an important area for migrating and nesting birds.*

MAP P42, D3

www.icnf.pt

Praia do Barril

From the village of Pedras del Rei (27km northeast of Faro and 5km southwest of Tavira), cross a narrow bridge to the long island Ilha de Tavira, then walk 1.5km or take the little train (€3 return). At the other end you'll find a glorious beach and the remnants of an old fishing settlement, with a bar-restaurant and a cemetery of anchors from the former tuna fleet.

Ilha da Armona

This large island has some fairly deserted stretches of sand at its eastern end, and a more sociable family-oriented scene at its western end, where there's a campsite and a village, the residents of which make their living harvesting shellfish in the estuary. You can reach the island by boat from Faro, Fuzeta or Olhão, or even wade across in places at low tide.

Kayaking

With calm waterways, offshore beaches and hidden corners, the Ria Formosa park is the ideal place to explore by kayak. Several operators, including Lands (p45), arrange hire and guided trips.

Birdwatching

These tidal wetland habitats support a great variety of birdlife, including many seabirds and waders, from flamingos to the emblem of the park, the purple gallinule. In winter it's home to over 20,000 birds; a great number of migratory species also stop over here in spring and autumn. Several companies run dedicated birdwatching boat tours; kayaking is another good way to spot avian life.

★ Top Tips

- Take care around the ends of the islands, where the estuary meets the sea, as there can be strong currents.
- Boat cruises from Faro or Tavira are a great way to get a feel for the park's geography and ecosystems.

Take a Break

Most of the islands have some eating and drinking options; little Fuzeta, a gateway to the Ilha da Armona, has a couple of outdoor places grilling seafood by the fish market building.

Faro and Tavira have the widest choice of shops to stock up on picnic ingredients.

Walking Tour

Historic Faro

The Algarve's capital been in the tourism spotlight since its international airport opened in the 1960s, but its history dates back millennia. On this walk, you'll explore its walled old town, visit centuries-old churches, and ascend towers for a bird's-eye perspective of the town and the glorious Ria Formosa's lagoons and islands offshore.

Walk Facts

Start Faro Marina

End Igreja de Nossa Senhora do Carmo & Capela dos Ossos

Length 2km; three hours

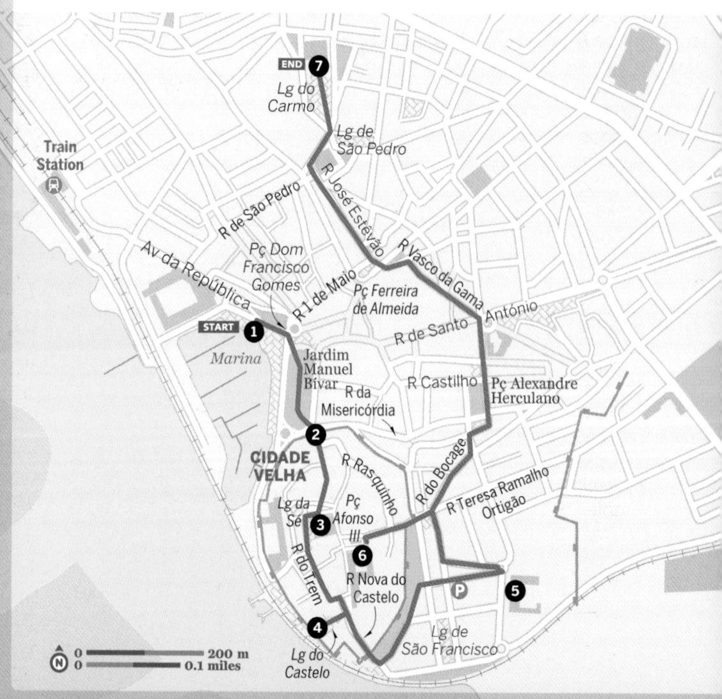

❶ Faro Marina

This is where it all began. **Faro's marina** lies on the Ria Formosa's lagoons, which served as a source of food and protection since at least Neolithic times. Today, the marina is the jumping-off point for cruises and kayaking trips to the protected Parque Natural da Ria Formosa's wildlife-filled waterways and islands.

❷ Old Town Gate

Opposite the 16th-century church Igreja da Misericórdia, enter Faro's walled old town, the *cidade velha*, through the **Arco da Vila** (Rua da Misericórdia 8; admission free; ⏲tower 9am-6pm). This neo-classical gate was built in 1812 under Bishop Francisco Gomes do Avelar, who oversaw the city's reconstruction after the 1755 earthquake. The tower above has an exhibition and great views from the top.

❸ Divine Views

More great views extend from the tower of Faro's **Sé** (p36). The cathedral has been built (and rebuilt) in a melange of styles over the centuries since it was initially completed back in the 13th century, likely on the site of a Roman temple. From the top, you can see out over the walls to the Ria Formosa beyond.

❹ Wall-Top Cafe

Take a break at Faro's most uniquely situated cafe, atop the old town's walls. A hybrid bar, restaurant, club and performance space, **O Castelo** (p49) has a terrace that morphs into a summer party space, and it hosts regular fado (traditional Portuguese song) performances by night.

❺ Monastic Church

Faro's monastery church **Igreja de São Francisco** (p44) had its foundations laid in 1679. Its spectacular baroque interior features traditional, hand-painted *azulejo* tiles. Part of the monastery now houses the Algarve's tourism and hospitality school.

❻ Archaeological Finds

Dig deep into Faro's past at the **Museu Municipal** (p43), housed in the domed 16th-century Renaissance Convento de Nossa Senhora da Assunção, in the former Jewish quarter. Artefacts unearthed in the local area and now displayed here date to the 3rd century.

❼ Baroque Beauty

End at the twin-towered baroque church **Igreja de Nossa Senhora do Carmo & Capela dos Ossos** (p43), dating from 1719, with its ornate interior and extraordinary bone chapel, constructed from the bones of 1000-plus monks, at the back.

A
B
C
D
1
2
3
4
5
6
Faro (7km)
R Aboim Ascenção
R do Alportel
R General Teófilo da Trindade
R de Loulé
R da Atalaia
Igreja de Nossa Senhora do Carmo & Capela dos Ossos
R Infante Dom Henrique
R Serpa Pinto
Lg do Carmo
R do Alportel
R Sotto Mayor
R Cruz dos Mestres
Lg de São Pedro
R Teófilo Braga
Lg do Estação
R Francisco Barreto
Igreja de São Pedro
R do Viola
R Gil Eanes
R do Forno
R de São Pedro
R Batista Lopes
R Dr Justino Cumano
Train Station
R da Bargueta
R Conselheiro de Bívar
R do Prior
R do Compromisso
R Filipe Alistão
R José Estêvão
R Lethes
R de Portugal
R da Mota
Parque Natural da Ria Formosa
Buses for Aeroporto de Faro & Praia de Faro
Av da República
Tv da Mota
R Vasco da Gama
R 1 de Maio
Pç Ferreira de Almeida
R de Santo António
Formosamar
Pç Dom Francisco Gomes
R Dom F Gomes
Museu Regional do Algarve
R do Pé da Cruz
Parque Natural da Ria Formosa
Marina
R Rebelo da Silva
Jardim Manuel Bívar
R Castilho
R Alexandre Herculano
Praça Alexandre Herculano
Igreja da Misericórdia
R da Misericórdia
R do Albergue
R Rasquinho
R de São Francisco
R do Bocage
R Teresa Ramalho Ortigão
CIDADE VELHA
R Comandante Francisco Manuel
Lg da Sé
Sé
Pç Dom Afonso III
R Caçadores 4
R do Repouso
R da Porta Nova
R do Trem
Museu Municipal
Animaris
R do Castelo
Igreja de São Francisco
Ilha da Barreta
Galeria Trem
Lg do Castelo
Lg de São Francisco
R Nova do Castelo
Ilha da Culatra
For reviews see
Top Experiences p36
Experiences p43
Eating p46
Drinking p49
Entertainment p50
Shopping p50
0 200 m
0 0.1 miles
N

Experiences

Igreja de Nossa Senhora do Carmo & Capela dos Ossos

CHURCH

1 MAP P42, C2

One of the Algarve's most dazzling churches, this twin-towered Baroque masterpiece was completed in 1719 under João V. After the 1755 earthquake, its spectacular facade was paid for with Brazilian gold, and the interior is gilded to the extreme, with numerous cherubs. Accessed through the church at the back, the 19th-century **Capela dos Ossos** is built from the bones and skulls of over 1000 monks as a reminder of earthly impermanence. It's quite a sight. (www.diocese-algarve.pt; Largo do Carmo; €2; church 9am-6pm Mon-Fri, 9am-1pm Sat Jun-Sep, 9am-5pm Mon-Fri, 9am-1pm Sat Oct-May, chapel 10am-1pm & 3-5.30pm Mon-Fri, 10am-1pm Sat year-round)

Museu Municipal

MUSEUM

2 MAP P42, C5

Faro's domed 16th-century Renaissance Convento de Nossa Senhora da Assunção, in what was once the Jewish quarter, houses the town's local history museum. Highlights include the 3rd-century *Mosaic of the Ocean*, found in 1976; 9th- to 13th-century domestic Islamic artefacts; and works by a notable Faro painter, Carlos Filipe Porfírio, depicting local legends. English-language leaflets detail key exhibits, including the *Paths of the Roman Algarve*, displaying

Capela dos Ossos

monumental Roman-laid stones. The museum hosts regular fado performances. (☎289 870 827; www.cm-faro.pt; Praça Dom Afonso III 14; adult/child €2/free; ⌚10am-7pm Mon-Fri, 11.30am-6pm Sat & Sun Jun-Sep, 10am-6pm Mon-Fri, 10.30am-5pm Sat & Sun Oct-May)

Igreja de São Francisco CHURCH

3 MAP P42, D5

The foundations of this monastery's church were laid in 1679 and it was enlarged during the 18th and 19th centuries. Behind its blinding white facade are dazzling woodwork and a frenzied 18th-century baroque interior with hand-painted *azulejo* tiles on the walls and a barrel-vaulted ceiling depicting the life of St Francis. (www.faro.ofs.pt; Largo de São Francisco; ⌚8am-7pm)

Museu Regional do Algarve MUSEUM

4 MAP P42, D3

Three of the four halls at this worthwhile museum house exhibitions on rural life in the Algarve, including mock-ups of 19th-century shops and rooms: a real fishing boat; some impressively woven creations in wicker, bamboo and palm leaves; and lots of rag rugs and fishing nets. The fourth hall is always given over to a temporary show on a folksy local theme. (☎289 870 893; www.cm-faro.pt; Praça da Liberdade 2; adult/child €1.50/free; ⌚10am-1.30pm & 2.30-6pm Mon-Fri)

Praia de Faro BEACH

5 MAP P42, A1

On the Ilha de Faro, 9km west of the centre, the town's beach has sweeping sand, windsurfing and kitesurfing operators, and a handful of cafes. It's crammed in high summer. Take bus 14 or 16 from the bus station (€2.30, 20 minutes, up to two per hour daily July to September, hourly Monday to Friday only October to June). (Ilha de Faro)

Igreja de São Pedro CHURCH

6 MAP P42, C2

While the exterior of this 16th-century church is unassuming, the tri-nave interior has magnificent 18th-century *azulejos* and intricately carved woodwork, including a rococo altar. (www.paroquiasaopedro-faro.org; Largo de São Pedro; ⌚8.30am-12.30pm & 3-7pm Mon-Sat, 9.30am-noon Sun)

Galeria Trem GALLERY

7 MAP P42, C5

This converted military warehouse displays contemporary art with temporary exhibitions by local and international artists – painters, photographers, installation artists and sculptors. There's no permanent collection, so It's worth popping by to see what's on. (www.cm-faro.pt; Rua do Trem 5; admission free; ⌚12.30-7pm Tue-Fri, 11.30am-6pm Sat Jun-Sep, 11.30am-6pm Tue-Fri, 10.30am-5pm Sat Oct-May)

Centro Histórico Judaico de Faro CEMETERY, MUSEUM

8 MAP P42, D1

The last vestiges of the first post-Inquisition Jewish presence in Portugal are found at this small Jewish cemetery. In use between 1838 and 1932, and restored in 1992, it has 76 beautiful marble gravestones. The site also has a tiny museum and recreated synagogue (complete with a reconstructed wedding and bar mitzvah). You're shown a DVD (in English), then given a detailed, interesting tour. It's behind the football stadium Estádio de São Luis, 1.3km northeast of the centre. (Faro Jewish Heritage Centre; 289 829 525; www.cm-faro.pt; Estrada da Penha; admission by donation; 9.30am-12.30pm & 2-5pm Mon-Fri)

Igreja da Misericórdia CHURCH

9 MAP P42, C4

The 16th-century Igreja da Misericórdia, opposite the Arco da Vila, was originally built in Manueline (Portuguese late Gothic) style but is now nearly all baroque after the destruction caused by the 1755 earthquake. (www.diocese-algarve.pt; Praça Dom Francisco Gomes 17; 9am-6pm Mon-Sat Jun-Sep, to 5pm Mon-Sat Oct-May)

Formosamar CRUISE, KAYAKING

10 MAP P42, B3

This recommended outfit promotes environmentally responsible tourism. Among its excellent tours are two-hour birdwatching trips around the Parque Natural da Ria Formosa (€25), dolphin watching (€45), cycling (€37) and a two-hour kayak tour negotiating some of the narrower lagoon channels (€35). All trips have a minimum number of participants (usually two to four). (918 720 002; www.formosamar.com; Avenida da República, Stand 1, Faro Marina)

Animaris CRUISE

11 MAP P42, B5

Animaris runs trips to Ilha da Barreta. Ferries take 45 minutes, while speedboats zip across in 15 minutes. Animaris also runs year-round guided boat trips through Parque Natural da Ria Formosa, dropping you at the island to return by ferry or speedboat at your own pace. Boats leave from the pier next to Arco da Porta Nova. (918 779 155; www.ilha-deserta.com; Rua Comandante Francisco Manuel; return ferry/speedboat €5/10, 1hr boat trip from €27.50; 10am-4.45pm)

Lands TOURS

Lands (see 10 Map p42, B3) runs 45-minute solar boat tours (€15), two-hour kayak tours (€35) and guided walks including birdwatching (from €120 for up to four people), all with an environmental slant. It also hires out kayaks (half-/full day €35/45) for you to explore Ria Formosa on your own. Four-hour sailing trips for up to six people cost €400. (914 539 511; www.lands.pt; Avenida da República, Stand 3, Faro Marina)

Sustainable Tourism in the Algarve

Much of Portugal's tourism income comes from the Algarve. Local visitors compose a large part of the industry – numerous Portuguese have homes in this sun-kissed region – and many expats have moved here permanently. The influx has led to ongoing heavy development along much of the Algarve's southern coastline.

While the Algarve's tourism industry provides work – albeit seasonal – to thousands of people, especially the young, some argue that the departure of Portuguese from their villages has caused irreversible disintegration of traditions and village life. Concerns have also been raised about the environmental impact of large (mainly concrete) hotels and apartments, and major roads, as well as the destruction of coastal areas (including cliffs and beaches), and pressure on water resources.

Tourism authorities have now focused their efforts on promoting special-interest activities beyond sun, surf and sand, instead highlighting the region's spectacular nature, walks and inland villages.

When visiting the Algarve, think carefully about the impact of your visit on this sensitive region: head inland (responsibly), be selective about the enterprises you choose and consider the impact of the activities you undertake.

Natura Algarve

CRUISE

This ecoresponsible operator (see 10 Map p42, B3) offers a range of trips, from all-day tours exploring the Ria Formosa (€52 excluding lunch, 5½ hours) to two-hour dolphin trips (€45), 2½-hour birdwatching trips (€35) and the popular 'Natura' trip – a 3½-hour interpretative tour covering history, traditions and the local economy (€30), exploring the canals as well as nearby Ilha da Culatra. (918 056 674; www.natura-algarve.com; Avenida da República, Stand 2, Faro Marina)

Eating

Vila Adentro

PORTUGUESE €€

12 MAP P42, C5

With tables on the square in Faro's old town and a dining room decorated with floor-to-ceiling *azulejos*, this Moorish 15th-century building is a romantic spot for elevated Portuguese cuisine: pork, clam and lobster *cataplanas* (stew) for two, chargrilled octopus with fig and carob sauce, and tangerine-stuffed pork filet. Wines hail from around the country. (933 052 173; www.vilaadentro.pt; Praça Dom Afonso

III 17; mains €9-17.50, cataplanas €39-49; 9am-midnight;)

Faz Gostos

PORTUGUESE €€€

13 MAP P42, C5

Sophisticated twists on Portuguese classics at this stylish restaurant in the old town might include *xarém* (corn porridge) with Ria Formosa clams, steamed sea bass with olive oil–poached potatoes, cornbread-topped cod, or chorizo-stuffed pork loin with fig sauce, depending on what's in season. Presentation is exquisite. The cellar has over 250 Portuguese wines. (914 133 668; www.fazgostos.com; Rua do Castelo 13; mains €12-25; noon-3pm & 6.30-10pm Sun-Fri, 6.30-10pm Sat;)

Restaurante Madeirense

MADEIRAN €€

14 MAP P42, C4

For an exotic take on Portuguese cuisine, this small Madeiran restaurant bangs down plates loaded with specialities you'll only get on the Island of Eternal Spring. *Espada* (scabbard fish), *bolo de caco* (potato bread) and *pudim de maracuja* (passionfruit pudding) are just some of the treats on offer; round things off with a *poncha* (sugar-cane liqueur) or sweet Madeira wine. (967 168 140; www.facebook.com/restaurantemadeirensefamilia; Rua 1 Dezembro 28; mains €8-17; noon-10.30pm Tue-Sun)

Faro Marina (p41)

Island Dining

Built to look like a crab when viewed from above, remote seafood restaurant **Estaminé** (☎917 811 856; www.estamine.deserta.pt; Ilha da Barreta; mains €18-28; ⏲10am-6pm) rises up on boardwalks from the Ilha da Barreta as its sole building. It's an entirely self-sufficient operation, using 100% solar power and desalinated water. Fresh-as-it-gets seafood dishes span Ria Formosa oysters, cracked crab and lobster to chargrilled prawns and fish, and aromatic stews. It's owned by Animaris (p45), which operates the ferry service here.

A Venda PORTUGUESE €

15 MAP P42, C3

Homestyle Portuguese food at bargain prices – Monchique blood sausage stew; fava bean fritters with smoked paprika sauce – and a retro interior with an ancient tiled floor, mismatched furniture and antique glass display cases make this backstreet place a red-hot favourite with local students. DJs often spin on summer nights. (Rua Do Compromisso 60; dishes €4-9; ⏲1-3pm & 7.30-11pm Tue-Sat)

Maktostas CAFE €

16 MAP P42, C2

Students and bohemians head to the tree-shaded terrace of this laid-back hang-out for chargrilled seafood and meats, traditional stews, plentiful vegan and vegetarian dishes including tofu steaks, bean burgers and enormous rusks (aka toasties), or just a few beers. It overlooks a peaceful square. (☎916 300 517; Rua do Alportel 29; dishes €2.50-12.50; ⏲kitchen 8am-11pm, bar to 2am;)

Gengibre e Canela VEGETARIAN €

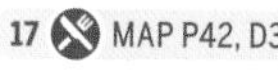

17 MAP P42, D3

Arrive early before this cosy spot fills to capacity (it doesn't take reservations) and its all-you-can-eat vegetarian buffet starts running low. Each day there are four main dishes (including a couple of curries) along with salads; wine and desserts are extra. Cash only. (Travessa da Mota 10; buffet €7.50; ⏲noon-3pm Mon-Sat;)

Restaurante O Murta SEAFOOD €€

18 MAP P42, A1

This simple place has been here for decades, so it must be doing something right. It grills quality meat and fish, and prepares excellent seafood dishes such as *açorda de marisco* (seafood stew in a bread bowl) and its signature *bacalhau* (salt-cod) dish, prepared with piri-piri and chilli, as well as *cataplanas* for two. (☎289 823 480; www.facebook.com/OMurta; Rua Infante Dom Henrique 136; mains €8-13.50, cataplanas €25-35; ⏲noon-3.30pm & 7.30-10.30pm Mon-Sat)

Adega Nova

PORTUGUESE €€

19 MAP P42, A2

With a menu of simply grilled fish and meat, this popular place has plenty of country charm, with a beamed ceiling, rustic cooking implements on display and seating over two levels, including long, communal tables, creating one of Faro's most atmospheric dining rooms. All wines on the extensive list are Portuguese. (289 813 433; www.restauranteadeganova.com; Rua Francisco Barreto 24; mains €11-16.50; 11.30am-11pm;)

Drinking

O Castelo

BAR

20 MAP P42, C5

O Castelo is all things to all people: bar, restaurant, club and performance space. Its location atop the old town walls provides stunning Ria Formosa views, especially at sunset. Beers, wine and cocktails are accompanied by tapas such as flambéed chorizo and local cheeses. (www.facebook.com/OCasteloBar.CidadeVelha.Faro; Rua do Castelo 11; 10.30am-4am Wed-Mon;)

A Short History of Faro

After hosting the Phoenicians and Carthaginians, Faro boomed as the Roman port Ossonoba. During the Moorish occupation it became the cultured capital of an 11th-century principality.

Afonso III took the town in 1249 – making it the last major Portuguese town to be recaptured from the Moors – and walled it.

Portugal's first printed works – books in Hebrew made by a Jewish printer – came from Faro in 1487.

A city from 1540, Faro had a brief golden age that ground to a halt in 1596 during Spanish rule. Troops under the Earl of Essex, en route to England from Spain in 1597, plundered the city and carried off hundreds of priceless theological works from the bishop's palace, now part of the Bodleian Library in Oxford.

Battered Faro was rebuilt, only to be shattered by an earthquake in 1722 and then almost flattened by another in 1755, though the historic centre largely survived. In 1834 Faro became the Algarve's capital.

The opening of the airport in 1965 established Faro as an international gateway to the region. Its passenger terminal opened in 1989 ahead of the early-21st-century arrival of low-cost airlines. It was expanded in 2017, and in 2018 saw more than eight million passengers, further boosting Algarve tourism.

Columbus Bar
BAR

21 MAP P42, C4

In the heart of town, this Faro hotspot has a paved terrace and seating by the central square, and a vast, vaulted-brick interior. House-speciality cocktails include Chiquérrima (*medronho* brandy, lime, mint and ginger beer) and the Speakeasy (Madeira rum, Grand Marnier and cinnamon syrup). It gets lively from around 11pm. (www.barcolumbus.pt; Praça Dom Francisco Gomes 13; 4pm-2am Sun-Thu, to 4am Fri & Sat;)

Bar CheSsenta
BAR

22 MAP P42, B3

A miracle of split-levelling has managed to fit two floors, toilets and a stage for live music (mainly indie) into this tiny space in the heart of Faro's bar zone. Illustrations of Che Guevara cover the walls inside and out. (Rua do Prior 24; 5pm-4am;)

Entertainment

Teatro Lethes
THEATRE

23 MAP P42, D2

Faro's tiny and exquisite Italianate theatre hosts drama, music and dance performances. Adapted into a theatre in 1874 (from a building dating back to 1603), it was once the Jesuit Colégio de Santiago Maior. Check its website or ask the tourist office for a list of what's on; you can buy tickets online (though you'll need to print them). (289 878 908; www.actateatro.org.pt/teatrolethes; Rua de Portugal 58; box office 2-6pm Tue-Fri, 8-9.30pm performance days)

Shopping

Chocolates de Beatriz
CHOCOLATE

24 MAP P42, D4

Chocolates made in Odemira in the neighbouring Alentejo region are enticingly displayed in glass cabinets at this little shop. Dark, milk and white chocolates have fillings such as Portuguese-harvested sea salt, fig paste, *medronho* (strawberry-tree liqueur) or Algarve oranges. Walk through and you'll find a tiny cafe where you can sit down for a hot chocolate and treats on-site. (289 820 358; www.chocolatesdebeatriz.com; Rua Veríssimo de Almeida 5; 10am-1pm & 3-7pm Tue-Sat)

Mercado Municipal de Faro
MARKET

25 MAP P42, D2

Faro's modern covered market building makes a great place to wander, people-watch, buy fresh produce, sit down on a terrace with a coffee or have lunch at one of several restaurants here, such as **O Palhacinho** (mains €7.50-12.50; 7am-11pm Mon-Fri, to 4pm Sat;). (www.mercadomunicipaldefaro.pt; Largo Dr Francisco Sá Carneiro; stalls 7am-3pm Mon-Sat;)

Roman mosaic at Milreu

A Trip to Estói

Charming Estói, 10km northeast of Faro, centres on a pretty square dominated by a 16th-century church. It's best known for its 18th-century rococo palace and gardens, which have been renovated into a *pousada* (upmarket inn), the **Pousada do Palácio de Estoi** (www.pousadas.pt), on Rua São José. Nonguests can visit its magnificent public areas and gardens. Nearby is the wonderful artisan food and craft shop **Loja Canastra** (p55).

Situated 850m west of the village are the Roman **ruins** (289 997 823; www.monumentosdoalgarve.pt; Rua de Faro; adult/child €2/free; 10.30am-1pm & 2-6.30pm May-Sep, 9.30am-1pm & 2-5pm Oct-Apr) at Milreu. The ruins are so large and grand they were originally thought to have been a town. The villa, inhabited from the 1st century AD, has the characteristic peristyle form, with a gallery of columns around a courtyard. The highlight is the temple devoted to a water deity, the fish mosaics and former central pool. At the entrance is a small museum with a scale model of the temple in its glory days.

Eva buses (www.eva-bus.com) link Estói with Faro (€3.35, 25 minutes, 10 daily Monday to Friday, five Saturday, three Sunday).

Walking Tour

Olhão: a Fishing Town

The traditional port town of Olhão, 9km east of Faro, provides a wonderful and easily accessible opportunity to explore some of the more traditional aspects of Algarvian life. With its century-old market buildings, fishing heritage and down-to-earth vibe, it offers an earthy contrast to many of the coast's glitzier resorts.

Getting There

Olhão is 10km east of Faro.

(€1.45, 10 minutes, 10 daily)

(€3.35, 20 minutes, up to two per hour)

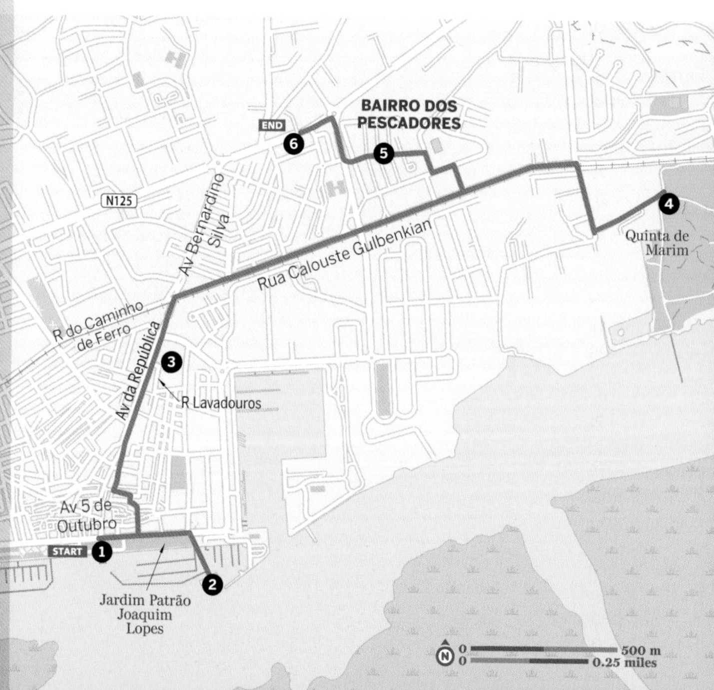

❶ Waterside Markets

By the water in the centre of Olhão, these two noble centenarian red-brick **buildings** (Avenida 5 de Outubro; ⏲7am-2pm Mon-Sat) are excellent examples of industrial architecture and house picturesque traditional fruit and fish markets that are great for nosing around. A string of simple seafood stalls and cafes makes them an atmospheric spot for a bite with water views.

❷ Island Beaches

Olhão is separated from the ocean by the islands and estuaries of the Parque Natural da Ria Formosa. **Ferries** (Avenida 5 de Outubro) to the islands depart year-round from the pier just east of Jardim Patrão Joaquim Lopes to the island beaches of Armona, Culatra and Farol. Zip across to soak up some sun or explore the little fishing hamlets.

❸ Local Lunch

The white, modern interior of **Tacho à Mesa** (☎961 624 577; www.facebook.com/tachoamesaolhao; Rua dos Lavadouros 46; mains €7-15, cataplanas €28-34; ⏲11am-3pm Mon, 11am-3pm & 7.30-10.30pm Tue-Sat, closed Jan; 📶), set back from main drag Avenida da República, plays host to some excellent traditional cooking with a cordial welcome to accompany it. With fresh produce purchased twice a day, it makes a great *cataplana* (seafood stew), super-juicy *bochechas* (pork cheeks) and other Algarvian-Alentejan delights.

❹ Nature Stroll

Perfect for walking off lunch, 2.5km east of Olhão is the beautiful 60-hectare **Quinta de Marim** (www.natural.pt; Quelfes; ⏲8am-8pm Mon-Fri, 10am-8pm Sat & Sun Jun-Sep 9am-noon & 2-5pm daily Oct-May), where a 3km nature trail takes you through various ecosystems – dunes, saltmarshes, pine woodlands – as well as to a wildlife rescue centre and a historic water mill. The Parque Natural da Ria Formosa headquarters and environmental centre are also here.

❺ Bairro dos Pescadores

This fisher's quarter, to the northeast of the centre, is a knot of whitewashed, cubical houses, often with tiled fronts and flat roofs for drying nets. Narrow lanes thread through the *bairro* (neighbourhood), and there's a definite Moorish influence, probably a legacy of long-standing trade links with North Africa.

❻ Vivenda Vitória

Heading back into town, at first glance this looks like a ruined church with a bell tower, but the Vivenda Vitória is in fact the elaborate early-20th-century home of a fish-canning magnate. It's now in a ruinous state; to replace the ugly scrawls that disfigured it, the council chose to commission a major graffiti project on its walls.

Driving Tour

Artisan Algarve

The Algarve's artisan traditions and innovations are showcased on this driving tour from Faro. Along the route, you'll taste handcrafted Portuguese chocolate, visit a groundbreaking craft brewery, watch tiles being hand-painted, tour a cork factory and an olive grove, and end the day sipping celebrated Portuguese wines from the region and beyond.

Drive Facts

Start Faro

End Faro

Length 155km; six hours

1 Craft Brewery

On Faro's industrial outskirts, **Algarve Rock** (289 815 203; www.algarverock.com; Unidade B, Parq Vale da Venda; 9am-5pm Mon-Fri) brews (and sells) organic, preservative-free, vegan brews inspired by the region, such as piri-piri pilsner and carob stout.

2 Hand-Painted Ceramics

Watch artists hand-painting traditional *azulejo* tiles at **Porches Pottery** (282 352 858; www.porchespottery.com; N125, Porches; 9am-6pm Mon-Fri, 10am-2pm Sat), whose ceramics span plates, bowls, vases, lamps and pots. Clad in classic blue-and-white tiles and opening to a bougainvillea-draped terrace, its cafe serves quiches, salads and cakes on its own crockery.

3 Cork Factory

On a fascinating behind-the-scenes 90-minute tour of cork factory **Nova Cortiça** (289 840 150; www.novacortica.pt; Parque Industrial da Barracha; tour €12.50; tours by reservation 10am-3.30pm Mon-Fri), you'll learn about the tree's life cycle, harvesting and the manufacturing process, from drying to the production of wine and champagne corks. It also showcases cork clothing, footwear and furniture.

4 Local Specialities

In the pretty village of Estói, browse jams, chutneys, preserves, honeys, olive oils, carob powder and products, dried herbs, tinned fish, wines and liqueurs (including carob, fig, almond and strawberry-tree varieties), plus handcrafted wooden chopping boards, at **Loja Canastra** (www.facebook.com/canastraestoi; Rua do Pé da Cruz 59; 10.30am-2pm & 3-7pm Tue-Fri, 10am-2.30pm Sat).

5 Olive Oil

Hour-long tours at gold medal–winning olive oil producer **Monterosa** (289 790 441; www.monterosa-oliveoil.com; Horta do Felix, Moncarapacho; tours adult/child €7/3.50; tours by reservation 10am Tue-Fri) take you around the 20-hectare estate's five different varieties of olive trees that are handpicked in autumn. You'll also see the Roman-era press in a granite mill where olives are ground before extraction and filtering, ending with a tasting.

6 Wine Tasting

Finish at stylish Faro wine bar **Epicur** (914 614 612; www.epicur.wine; Rua Alexandre Herculano 22; 5pm-midnight Tue-Sat), which has over 250 wines (30 by the glass) representing Portugal's major wine regions, including the Algarve. Pair them with *presunto* (charcuterie), tinned fish, local cheeses and Ria Formosa oysters. There are regular meet-the-winemakers events; you can buy bottles to take home.

Explore Tavira & Around

Set on either side of the meandering Rio Gilão, Tavira's warren of cobblestone streets hiding leafy gardens and shady squares, small active fishing port and historic attractions including castle ruins and a Roman bridge make it one of the Algarve's most charming towns. Only 3km from the coast, Tavira is the launching point for Ilha de Tavira's sweeping, unspoilt beaches.

The Short List

- **Ponte Romana (p59)** *Snapping the classic photo of the Roman Bridge straddling the Rio Gilão.*
- **Igreja da Misericórdia (p64)** *Being awed by this 16th-century church, a masterpiece of Renaissance architecture.*
- **Castelo (p59)** *Unwinding in the peaceful botanic gardens at Tavira's ruined castle.*
- **Fado Com História (p68)** *Hearing haunting Portuguese fado (traditional song) and learning about its origins.*
- **Camera Obscura (p64)** *Surveying Tavira from this camera obscura atop a former water tower.*

Getting There & Around

Buses run to destinations including Faro and Lisbon, and Huelva and Seville in nearby Spain.

Frequent trains zip to Faro and Vila Real de Santo António by the Spanish border.

Tavira Map on p62

Ponte Romana (p59) CARON BADKIN/SHUTTERSTOCK ©

Walking Tour

Tavira Through the Ages

Tavira's history comes alive at every turn as you stroll the picturesque streets and riverbanks. On this walk, you'll encounter its many layers while checking out the town's Roman bridge, Islamic history museum, hilltop castle and archaeological excavations that date all the way back to the time of the Phoenicians.

Walk Facts

Start Ponte Romana

End Camera Obscura Tower

Length 850m; two hours

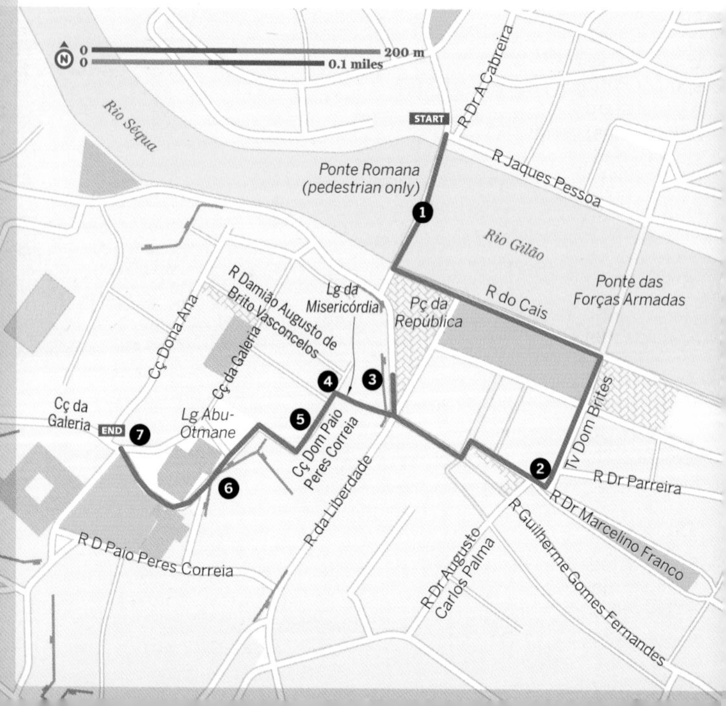

❶ Roman Bridge

Tavira's seven-arched Roman bridge, the **Ponte Romana**, may in fact predate the Romans. It's so named because it linked the Roman road from Castro Marim to Tavira. The structure you see dates from a 1667 reconstruction; it's been car-free since flood damage in 1989, but you can still cross it on foot.

❷ Local Pastries

Enduringly popular with its namesake *tavirense* (Tavira locals), **Pastelaria Tavirense** (Travessa Dom Brites; pastries €1.20-3.50; 7am-midnight;) is the ultimate spot for Portuguese *pastéis de nata* (custard-filled pastries), *bolos* (cakes), *tortas* (filled, rolled sponge) and *sonhos* (traditional doughnuts), along with strong coffee. You can dine on-site or take away.

❸ Islamic Finds

The contemporary museum **Núcleo Islâmico** (p63) is built around the remains of an Islamic-era structure. It exhibits impressive Islamic pieces discovered in the area. On the top floor, temporary exhibitions have a local theme.

❹ Renaissance Church

Constructed in 1520 when Dom Manuel I made Tavira a city, the stone archway Porta de Dom Manuel is one of the former city walls' few surviving sections. Beyond is the 16th-century **Igreja da Misericórdia** (p64), with restrained Renaissance arches. There's a museum and regular fado (traditional music) performances.

❺ Phoenician Ruins

Archaeological digs at the **Ruínas Fenícias de Tavira** (www.cm-tavira.pt; Calçada Dom Paio Peres Correia 4; admission free; 24hr) site have unearthed part of a Phoenician wall circa 800 BC, an ox-hide altar from the 4th century BC thought to be Turdetanian (the pre-Roman Iberian civilisation), Moorish foundations from the 12th century AD and a 17th-century Portuguese mansion.

❻ Age-Old Castle

High above the town is Tavira's ruined **castle** (Largo Abu-Otmane; admission free; 8am-5pm Mon-Fri, 9am-7pm Sat & Sun, to 5pm winter). Plausibly dating back to Neolithic times, the structure was rebuilt by Phoenicians and later taken over by the Moors; most of what now stands is a 17th-century reconstruction. The interior contains an exotic botanic garden. Take care, as the ramparts don't have railings.

❼ Water Tower Views

Once the town's water tower, the 100m-high Torre da Tavira now houses a panoramic **camera obscura** (p64) at the top.

Driving Tour

Along the Guadiana

Forming the border with Spain, the Rio Guadiana has plenty to offer along its banks, with castles, nature reserves, a riverside beach and a seaside town to explore. This drive makes a great day trip from Tavira and takes in some of the Algarve's lesser-visited corners.

Drive Facts

Start Tavira

End Tavira

Length 149km; four hours

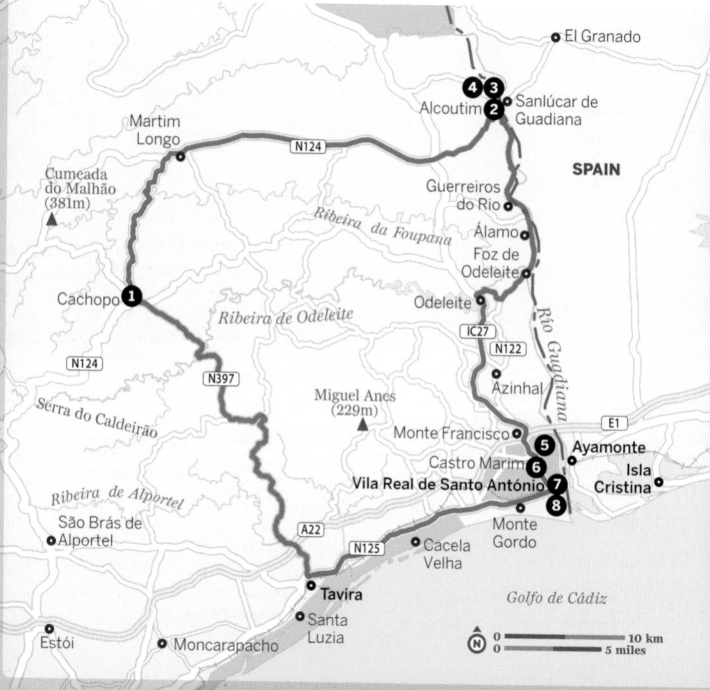

❶ Road to the Hills

It's a picturesque drive from Tavira north along the N397, which rises into the Algarve's hilly interior. The sweet village of **Cachopo** is a typical highland settlement, with steep, pin-drop-quiet streets.

❷ Alcoutim's Castle

The flower-ringed, 14th-century **castelo** (☎281 540 509; www.cm-alcoutim.pt; Largo do Castelo; €2.50; ⏲9.30am-7pm Jun-Aug, to 5.30pm Sep-May) at Alcoutim has sweeping views. Inside the grounds is an excellent archaeological museum, displaying ruined medieval castle walls and other artefacts.

❸ An Unusual Beach

Set on a bend in a narrow tributary of the Guadiana, Alcoutim's cute little riverside **Praia Fluvial** (www.cm-alcoutim.pt) is equipped with sand, a cafe, palm-leaf umbrellas and a lifeguard!

❹ Hearty Lunch

In the heart of Alcoutim, **O Camané** (Praça da República; mains €8-15; ⏲noon-2pm & 7.30-10pm Wed-Mon Jun-Aug, hours vary Sep-May) is a popular spot for Algarvian and Alentejan dishes like *porco preto* (Iberian pig) and *açorda* (bread soup).

❺ Birdwatchers' Wetland

Established in 1975, the **Reserva Natural do Sapal de Castro Marim** (www.cm-castromarim.pt; Sapal de Venta Moinhos, Apartado 7; ⏲9am-12.30pm & 2-5.30pm Mon-Fri) is mainland Portugal's oldest nature reserve, covering marshland and salt pans bordering the Rio Guadiana. Walking trails with interpretive signs fan out from the park's headquarters.

❻ Mighty Fortress

Much of the area around the small town of Castro Marim was destroyed in the 1755 earthquake, but the ruins of the huge **castle** (www.cm-castromarim.pt; Travessa do Castelo; adult/child €1.10/free; ⏲9am-7pm Apr-Sep, to 5pm Oct-Mar) complex are still amazing. Inside the walls is a 14th-century church, the Igreja de Santiago, where Prince Henry the Navigator is said to have prayed.

❼ Border Town

Staring across at Ayamonte in Spain over the Rio Guadiana, the small pedestrian centre of **Vila Real de Santo António** was designed on a grid pattern by the Marquês de Pombal after the town was destroyed by floods.

❽ Sundowner with a View

On the water side of the waterfront road in Vila Real, the **Associação Naval do Guadiana** (☎281 513 038; www.anguadiana.com; Avenida da República 25A; mains €14-40, cataplanas €36-38, seafood platters €70-130; ⏲noon-3pm & 6.30-10.30pm Wed-Mon; 📶) has the best views in town.

A B C D E F
1 2 3 4
0 200 m
0 0.1 miles

Rio Séqua
Rio Gilão
R Chefe António Afonso
R João Vaz Corte Real
R Borda d'Água da Assêca
Abílio Bikes
Pç Dr António Padinha
R Dr A Cabreira
R Dr Augusto Silva Carvalho
Tv Jaques Pessoa
Lg do Trem
Tv da Caracolinha
R Almirante Cândido dos Reis
R Poeta Emiliano da Costa
R José Joaquim Jara
R Comandante Henrique Brito
Tourist Train
R Jaques Pessoa
R Borda d'Água de Aguiar
R Gonçalo Velho
R dos Pelames
Ponte Romana (pedestrian only)
Praça da República
Ponte das Forças Armadas
Cç Dona Ana
Cç da Galeria
Lg da Misericórdia
Palácio da Galeria
Núcleo Islâmico
R do Cais
Mercado da Ribeira
Tv Dom Brites
Camera Obscura Tower
Lg Abu-Otmane
Porta de Dom Manuel
R dos Bombeiros Municipais
Igreja de Santa Maria do Castelo
Igreja de Santiago
R da Liberdade
Igreja da Misericórdia
R Dr Marcelino Franco
R Dr José Pires Padinha
R Dr Parreira
R António Viegas
R D Paio Peres Correia
R Guilherme Gomes Fernandes
R Montalvão
Tv do Garção
R 31 de Janeiro
R da Silva
R 1º de Maio
R Tenente Couto
R Dr Augusto Carlos Palma
R Dr Silvestre Falcão
R Dr Miguel Bombarda
Av Dr Teixeira de Azevedo
Pç Zacarias Guerreiro
R 25 de Abril
R Poço do Bispo
Av Dom Manuel I
(250m)
Santa Luzia (2.5km)
R do Poeta Isidoro Pires
Campo dos Mártires da Pátria
Biblioteca Municipal Álvaro de Campos

1 2 3 4 5 6 7 8 9 10 11 12 13 14 15 16 17 18 19 20 21 22 23 24 25 26 27

For reviews see

Experiences	p63
Eating	p67
Drinking	p69
Shopping	p69

Experiences

Igreja de Santa Maria do Castelo

CHURCH

1 MAP P62, B2

Built in Gothic style over a mosque, then rebuilt by an Italian neoclassicist following earthquake damage 500 years later, this church by the castle retains original elements – namely the main doorway, two side chapels and Arabic-style windows in the clock tower. Inside, a plaque marks the tomb of Dom Paio Peres Correia, who took the town back from the Moors, and those of the seven Christian knights whose killing by the Moors precipitated the final attack on Tavira. (www.diocese-algarve.pt; Calçada da Galeria; €2; 10am-1pm & 2-5pm Mon-Fri 10am-1pm Sat)

Núcleo Islâmico

MUSEUM

2 MAP P62, C2

Built around the remains of an Islamic-era structure, this small 21st-century museum exhibits impressive Islamic pieces discovered in various excavations around the old town. One of the most important finds on display is the Tavira vase, an elaborate ceramic work with figures and animals around the rim. Multilingual handouts are available at reception. The top floor of the museum is dedicated to temporary exhibitions with a local theme. (281 320 570; www.cm-tavira.pt; Praça da República 5; adult/child €2/1, with Palácio da Galeria €3/1.50; 9.15am-12.30pm & 1.30-4.30pm Tue-Sun)

Salt pans, Quatro Águas (p64)

Camera Obscura Tower

LANDMARK

3 MAP P62, B2

Rising 100m high, the **Torre da Tavira** was formerly the town's water tower and now houses a camera obscura at the top, reached by a lift. A simple but ingenious object, the camera obscura reveals a 360-degree panoramic view of Tavira, its monuments and local events, in real time – all while you remain stationary. (Torre da Tavira; www.torredetavira.com; Calçada da Galeria 12; adult/child €4/2; 10am-5pm Mon-Fri, to 1pm Sat Jul-Sep, 10am-5pm Mon-Fri Feb-Jun, to 4pm Oct-Jan)

Igreja da Misericórdia

CHURCH

4 MAP P62, C2

Built between 1541 and 1551, this church is the Algarve's most important Renaissance monument, with a magnificent carved, arched doorway. Inside, the restrained Renaissance arches contrast with the cherub-festooned baroque altar and enormous panels of *azulejos* (hand-painted tiles) depicting the works of mercy. Fado performances are sublime here. Behind is a museum with salvers, chalices, and a hall with an interesting 18th-century applewood ceiling and elegant furniture. (www.diocese-algarve.pt; Largo da Misericórdia; church incl museum €2, fado performances €8; 10am-12.30pm & 3-6.30pm Tue-Sat Jul & Aug, 9.30am-12.30pm & 2-5.30pm Tue-Sat Sep-Jun, fado performances 3.15pm Sat year-round)

Palácio da Galeria

MUSEUM

5 MAP P62, C2

With oyster-grey baroque window mouldings and 16 hipped, terracotta-tiled roofs, this whitewashed, 16th-century palace now hosts a variety of exhibitions on a wide range of artistic and historical topics. (Museu Municipal de Tavira; 281 320 540; www.cm-tavira.pt; Calçada da Galeria; adult/child €2/1, with Núcleo Islâmico €3/1.50; 10am-12.30pm & 3-6pm Tue-Sat Apr-Oct, 9.15am-4.30pm Tue-Sat Nov-Mar)

Porta de Dom Manuel

GATE

6 MAP P62, C2

Built in 1520 when Dom Manuel I made Tavira a city, this stone archway is one of the few surviving sections of the former city walls. (Largo da Misericórdia)

Quatro Águas

AREA

7 MAP P62, F3

You can walk 2km east along the river, past the fascinating, snowlike salt pans to Quatro Águas. The salt pans produce tip-top table salt and attract feeding birds in summer, including flamingos. It's the jumping-off point for ferries to Ilha de Tavira and has a couple of simple seafood restaurants.

Biblioteca Municipal Álvaro de Campos

ARCHITECTURE, LIBRARY

8 MAP P62, D4

Architecture buffs should pay a visit to Tavira's municipal library,

Azulejos (hand-painted tiles), Igreja da Misericórdia

which was originally the town prison. Architect João Luís Carrilho da Graça sympathetically converted the former prison's facade and cells into a modern, harmonious cultural space in 2005, which hosts occasional exhibitions. (☎281 320 585; www.cm-tavira.pt; Rua da Comunidade Lusíada 21; ⏲10.30am-5.30pm Mon-Fri Jul & Aug, 10am-6.30pm Tue-Fri, 2-6.30pm Mon & Sat Sep-Jun)

Praça da República SQUARE

9 MAP P62, C2

For centuries this town square on the riverfront served as a promenade and a marketplace, where slaves were traded along with fish and fruit. Today a large part has been remodelled as an amphitheatre, and is covered with tables that spill from the square's many cafes.

Igreja de Santiago CHURCH

10 MAP P62, B3

Just south of Tavira's castle is the whitewashed 17th-century Igreja de Santiago, thought to have been built where a small mosque once stood. The park beside it was formerly the Praça da Vila, the old town square. (www.diocese-algarve.pt; Rua Dom Paio Peres Correia; ⏲10am-1pm & 2-5pm Mon-Fri, 10am-1pm 1st Sat of month)

Arraial Ferreira Neto Museum MUSEUM

11 MAP P62, E1

Quaint displays at this tiny tuna-fishing museum include a diorama

Santa Luzia

The fishing village of **Santa Luzia** is effectively a district of Tavira these days, and it's a great place to wander to get a feel for typical Algarve life. Overlooking the channel that separates the mainland from the Ilha de Tavira, the village is famous for its *polvo* (octopus), which you can try in several restaurants. You'll often see fishers mending nets in their storage huts. Boat trips also leave from the waterfront here.

of the complex tuna-netting system, mannequins in period dress, model boats and black-and-white photos. (281 380 800; www.vilagale.com; Hotel Vila Galé Albacora, Quatro Águas; admission free; 9am-6pm Mar-Oct)

Passeios Ria Formosa CRUISE

12 MAP P62, F1

Wildlife-spotting cruises from Cabanas de Tavira, 6km east of Tavira, include an hour-long tour of the Ria Formosa protected area, a 90-minute flamingo-spotting tour and a four-hour octopus tour, stopping at Santa Luzia. The company also runs various boat trips departing directly from Santa Luzia, as well as Olhão and Fuseta. (962 156 922; www.passeios-ria-formosa.com; Avenida 28 de Maio, Cabanas de Tavira; 1hr cruise €12.50, 90min flamingo tour €20, 4hr octopus tour €30)

Kitesurf Eolis KITESURFING

13 MAP P62, F1

Based at Cabanas de Tavira this highly professional operator has kitesurfing classes, as well as 'kite-bugging' (land-yacht-style kiting along the sand, aka 'blokarting') and SUP (stand-up paddleboarding) lessons and equipment hire. (962 337 285; www.kitesurfeolis.com; Rua Capitão Baptista Marçal 41, Cabanas de Tavira; 4hr kitesurfing lesson €100, 2hr kitebugging €65)

Tourist Train TOURS

14 MAP P62, D1

Starting on the northern side of the Ponte Romana, this handy little tourist 'train' (on wheels) trundles between Tavira's main sights, including Quatro Águas (from where ferries run to Ilha de Tavira), Praça da República and the castelo. (289 389 067; www.delgaturis.com; 50min circuit adult/child €5/3, hop-on, hop-off day ticket €6/4; hourly 10am-9pm Jul-Sep, to 6pm Oct-Jun)

Abílio Bikes CYCLING

15 MAP P62, C1

Tavira's oldest bike shop rents out all kinds of bikes. Weekly discounts are available; staff can give advice on great rides in the area. (281 323 467; www.abiliobikes.com; Rua João Vaz Corte Real 23; per day city/mountain/electric bike €8/13/35; 9.30am-1pm & 3-7pm Mon-Sat

Jun-Oct, 9.30am-1pm & 3-7pm Mon-Fri, 9.30am-1pm Sat Nov-May)

Eating

O Tonel

PORTUGUESE €€

16 MAP P62, D1

Contemporary Portuguese cuisine is complemented by a striking dining room of scarlet walls and *azulejos*. Begin with *petiscos* (tapas) like chorizo sautéed in *medronho* (local brandy) or clam-and-mackerel pâté served in a tin with crusty bread, before moving on to mains such as almond-crusted pork or carob-marinated lamb. Wines come from all over Portugal. Book ahead. (963 427 612; Rua Dr Augo Silva Carvalho 6; tapas €3.50-7.50, mains €9-16; 6.30-10pm Mon-Sat)

Casa Simão

PORTUGUESE €

17 MAP P62, C1

Filled with locals, this old-style, family-run restaurant concentrates on honest, down-to-earth dishes such as *javali estufado* (wild-boar stew) and grilled fish and meat (served with coriander rice and tomato salad), plus, at lunch, a choice of three daily specials. (281 321 647; www.facebook.com/RestauranteSimao; Rua João Vaz Corte Real 10; mains €6-12; noon-2pm & 6-10pm Mon-Sat mid-Dec–Oct)

Luzzo Pizzeria

PIZZA €€

18 MAP P62, C1

Tuti trufi (truffle oil and black-truffle shavings), *siffredi* (with *ventricina* spicy sausage, rocket and balsamic) and the house

Praça da República (p65)

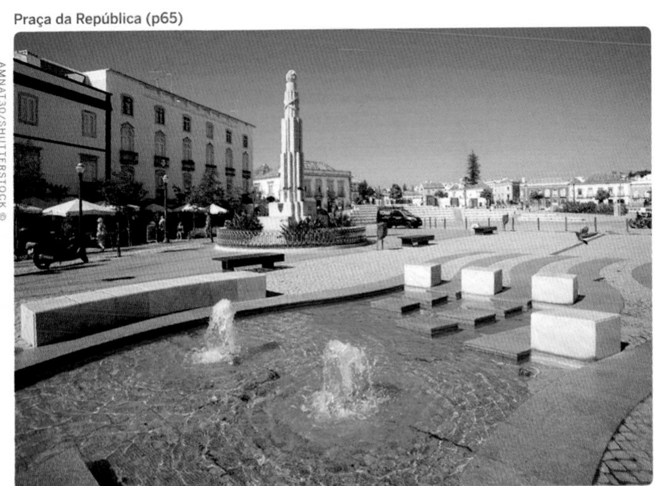

Traditional Fado

If you haven't experienced fado (traditional song), the comprehensive introduction at **Fado Com História** (966 620 877; www.fadocomhistoria.com; Rua Damião Augo de Brito Vasconcelos 4; adult/child €8/free; shows 12.15pm, 3.15pm & 5.15pm Mon-Fri, 12.15pm & 5.15pm Sat, museum 10am-6pm Mon-Sat) is even more worthwhile. Space is limited, so buy your ticket a couple of hours ahead. The 35-minute show begins with an interesting film about fado's roots and history, followed by three live songs with explanations in English. On Saturdays, the 3.15pm performance takes place at the Igreja da Misericórdia (p64).

speciality *luzzo* (portobello mushrooms, crispy bacon and caramelised pineapple) are just some of the enormous thin-crust pizzas pulled from the wood-fired oven at this fabulous spot. Dine in the plant-filled interior or pick up pizzas to take away. (281 327 016; www.facebook.com/luzzotavira; Rua João Vaz Corte Real 28; pizzas €7-15.75; noon-3pm & 7-11pm;)

Aquasul EUROPEAN €€

19 MAP P62, D1

Behind a rose-covered facade, mosaics and local artworks line the walls of this popular spot, while mismatched tables are topped in tiles, marble and brightly painted timbers. Dishes change seasonally and might include roast duck breast with port wine reduction, and porcini and white-truffle ravioli (around a quarter of the menu is vegetarian). (281 325 166; Rua Dr Augo Silva Carvalho 11; mains €9-20.50; 6.30-10pm Tue-Sat Mar–mid-Dec;)

A Barquinha PORTUGUESE €€

20 MAP P62, E3

One of the better choices on this restaurant-heavy riverside strip, this cluttered, narrow place is hospitable and cosy. Simple salads and grilled local fish are the way to go. Pavement tables overlook the water. (281 322 843; Rua Dr José Pires Padinha 142; mains €8-15; 12.30-3pm & 6-10pm Thu-Tue mid-Feb–Nov)

Restaurante Avenida PORTUGUESE €€

21 MAP P62, B4

This authentic Portuguese place with paper tablecloths has an air of the 1960s, efficiency with a capital 'E' and a loyal clientele. Consistently good homestyle dishes include *caldo verde* (potato, kale and chorizo soup), *pastéis de bacalhau* (cod fritters) and *caldeirada de peixe* (fish stew). (281 321 113; Praça Zacarias Guerreiro; mains €8-16; noon-3pm & 6.30-10pm Wed-Mon;)

Drinking

Pessoa's Cafe

BAR

22 MAP P62, D1

Abstract oils and watercolours cover the walls of Pessoa's, but in summer the best seats are on the sunny, south-facing riverside terrace, so get in early. Wines, beers and local liqueurs pair with *queijo* (cheese) and *charcutaria* platters. Acoustic or folk music occasionally plays. (www.facebook.com/PessoaSCafe; Rua Jacques Pessoa 22; noon-11pm Wed-Sun early Jan-Oct;)

Sítio Cafe

CAFE

23 MAP P62, D1

One of the few summer hotspots with any atmosphere out of season, Sítio is divided into three parts: outside, light-inside and neon-lit dark-inside. Drinks span house wine and beer to sangria and cocktails. During the day, stop by for a coffee or light meal. (www.facebook.com/sitiocafetavira; Largo do Trem; 8.30am-2am Mon-Thu, 8.30am-3am Fri, 6.30pm-3am Sat;)

Tavira Lounge

BAR

24 MAP P62, C2

By day it's a cafe-restaurant, by night a cafe-bar. At all times, it's a relaxed place to kick back with a smoothie or cocktail. Its inviting spaces include a contemporary timber-furnished interior, a glass-encased terrace and al fresco tables overlooking the river. (281 381 034; Rua Gonçalo Velho 16-18; noon-2am Mon-Sat Jun-Sep, reduced hours Oct-May;)

Ref

BAR

25 MAP P62, C2

Laid-back Ref has a lounge-like, 1970s feel but plays contemporary music. Punch is served in summer (when the action spills out into the laneway) and shots of local liqueurs such as carob or fig in winter, along with local beers and wines year-round. (Rua Gonçalo Velho 23; 10pm-3am daily Jul & Aug, 10pm-2am Thu, to 3am Fri & Sat Sep-Jun;)

Shopping

Garrafeira Soares

DRINKS

26 MAP P62, D2

Opposite the market building, this outlet of the Algarve liquor chain has a good selection of Portuguese wines, port and spirits. (www.garrafeirasoares.pt; Rua Dr José Pires Padinha 66; 10am-midnight Mon-Sat)

Mercado Municipal

MARKET

27 MAP P62, F4

Tavira's hangar-like modern food market near the bridge at the eastern edge of town sells fruit, vegetables, meat and fish. (www.cm-tavira.pt; Av Dom Manuel I; 7am-2pm Mon-Sat)

Worth a Trip
Cacela Velha

One of the Algarve's real beauty spots, the enchanting little cobbled village of Cacela Velha is a huddle of whitewashed cottages edged with bright borders, with a pocket-sized fort, orange and olive groves, and flower-filled gardens. Splendid views extend over the estuary to the ocean beyond, with a meandering path down to the waterside.

Igreja de Nossa Senhora da Assunção

The centrepiece of the village, like many of the Algarve's churches, has architectural features from a range of periods. Though the church dates from the 13th century, only a Gothic side door survives from the original construction. The interior conserves some Renaissance-era arches, while most of the rest is baroque, dating from both before and after the 1755 earthquake, which caused major damage.

Fortaleza

The village's fortress occupies a position that commands the coast in both directions and is still used by the National Republican Guard, so is not open to the public. Once a Moorish castle, it suffered various periods of decay and rebuilding; what you see today dates from the late 18th century. The walkway behind the church gives a good idea of the fortress' outlook.

Fábrica

A 1.4km drive west of Cacela Velha, or a lovely coastal stroll, brings you to the village of Fábrica, a tiny base for fisherfolk and shellfish pickers. It's a reminder that despite Cacela's jewel-like beauty, it's still a small traditional community.

Praia de Cacela Velha

Lonely and lovely, this bow-shaped spit of sand is divided from the mainland by an estuary. It can be reached by walking a couple of kilometres west from the beach at Manta Rota or by hiring a boat across the estuary from Fábrica. It's one of the least crowded of all the Algarve beaches; there's a low-key LGBTIQ+ scene here in summer.

★ Top Tips

- Visit early in the morning or late in the afternoon for serenity and the best light.
- Visitors need to park in the car park at the village entrance; village parking is residents only.
- These are people's homes, so be sensitive when taking pictures of those photogenic white houses.

✕ Take a Break

- In the heart of the village, **Casa da Igreja** (www.facebook.com/restaurantecasavelha; Rua de Cacela Velha 2; mains €9-15; ⌚noon-11pm daily Jul & Aug, noon-3pm & 7-10pm Tue-Sun Sep-Jun) is a very traditional *tasca* (tavern) near the church.
- Beachfront **A Fábrica do Costa** (☎281 951 467; Rua de Fábrica; mains €16-35, cataplanas €40-55; ⌚noon-3pm & 7-10.30pm Jun-Aug, hours vary Sep-May) in Fábrica specialises in seafood.

Instituto Superior Dom Afonso III

Loulé & Albufeira

One of the Algarve's largest inland towns, Loulé (lo-lay) is a busy commercial centre with an attractive old quarter, Moorish castle ruins, Roman history and artisans making wicker baskets, copperworks and embroidery. In complete contrast, party town Albufeira is awash with tourist-filled British pubs and bars, with beautiful outlying beaches, splashy water parks and activities galore.

The Short List

- ***Igreja de São Lourenço de Matos (p75)*** *Being mesmerised by this exquisite blue-and-white-tiled church in Almancil.*
- ***Mercado Municipal (p81)*** *Shopping for local delicacies at Loulé's magnificent art-nouveau market.*
- ***Fiesa (p78)*** *Marvelling at the creations at the world's largest sand-sculpture competition.*
- ***Nossa Senhora da Conceição (p75)*** *Visiting this picturesque chapel with a 3rd-century Islamic door.*
- ***Museu Municipal (p76)*** *Delving into Loulé's history at this castle-set museum.*

Getting There & Around

The bus station is on the town centre's northern edge. Daily connections include Albufeira, Faro and Lisbon.

Be aware that the station is 7km southwest of town (take any Quarteira-bound bus).

Loulé Map on p74

Dancers, Loulé old quarter

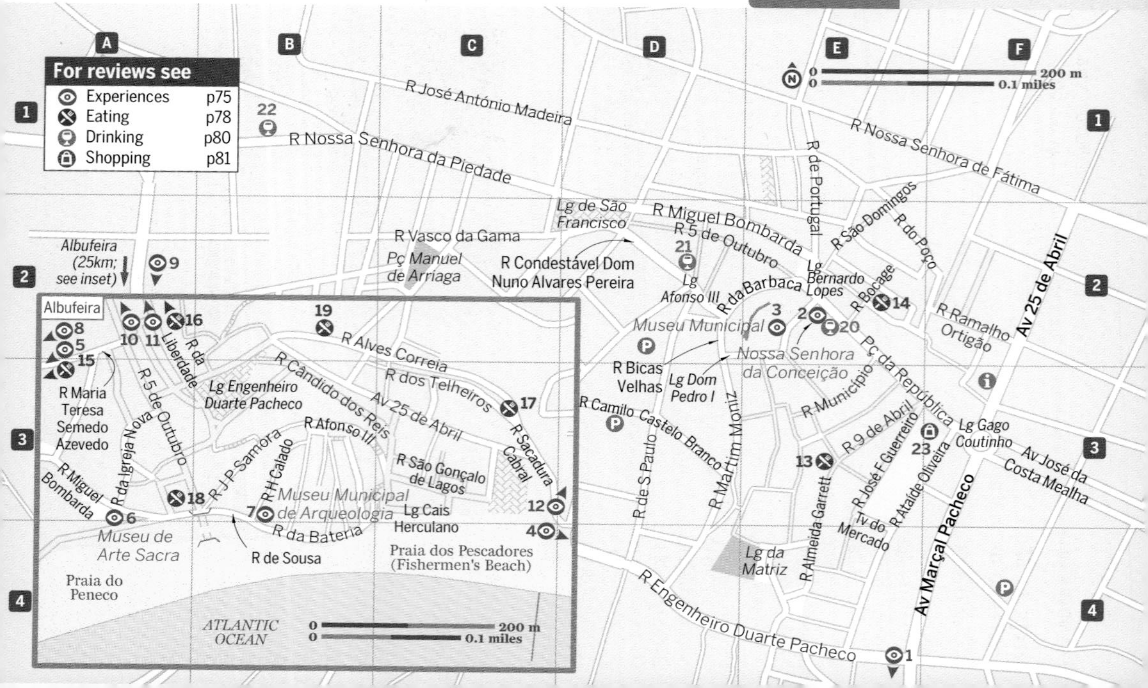

For reviews see

Experiences	p75
Eating	p78
Drinking	p80
Shopping	p81

A B C D E F
1 2 3 4
0 200 m
0 0.1 miles
R José António Madeira
R Nossa Senhora da Piedade
R Nossa Senhora de Fátima
R de Portugal
R São Domingos
R do Poço
Lg de São Francisco
R Miguel Bombarda
R 5 de Outubro
R Vasco da Gama
Pç Manuel de Arriaga
R Condestável Dom Nuno Alvares Pereira
Lg Afonso III
R da Barbaca
Lg Bernardo Lopes
R Bocage
R Ramalho Ortigão
Av 25 de Abril
Museu Municipal
Nossa Senhora da Conceição
Pç da República
R Bicas Velhas
Lg Dom Pedro I
R Camilo Castelo Branco
R Martim Moniz
R Município
R 9 de Abril
R de S Paulo
R Almeida Garrett
R José F Guerreiro
R Ataíde Oliveira
Tv do Mercado
Lg Gago Coutinho
Av José da Costa Mealha
Av Marçal Pacheco
Lg da Matriz
R Engenheiro Duarte Pacheco
Albufeira (25km; see inset)
Albufeira
R da Liberdade
R Alves Correia
R Cândido dos Reis
R dos Telheiros
Av 25 de Abril
Lg Engenheiro Duarte Pacheco
R Maria Teresa Semedo Azevedo
R 5 de Outubro
R da Igreja Nova
R Miguel Bombarda
R J P Samora
R H Calado
R Afonso III
R São Gonçalo de Lagos
R Sacadura Cabral
Museu Municipal de Arqueologia
Lg Cais Herculano
R da Bateria
R de Sousa
Museu de Arte Sacra
Praia do Peneco
Praia dos Pescadores (Fishermen's Beach)
ATLANTIC OCEAN
0 200 m
0 0.1 miles

Experiences

Igreja de São Lourenço de Matos CHURCH

1 MAP P74, E4

This baroque masterpiece was built on the site of a ruined chapel after locals, while digging a well, implored St Lawrence for help and then struck water. Constructed by brothers Antão and Manuel Borges, it's smothered in *azulejos* (hand-painted tiles) – even the ceiling – depicting the saint's life and death. In the 1755 earthquake, only five tiles fell from the roof. It's 9km south of Loulé; buses (€2.35, 15 minutes, up to two per hour) stop 2.5km west in Almancil's centre. (Church of St Lawrence of Rome; www.diocese-algarve.pt; Rua da Igreja, Almancil; €2; 10am-1pm & 3-6pm Mon, 3-6pm Tue-Sat)

Nossa Senhora da Conceição CHAPEL

2 MAP P74, E2

Situated opposite Loulé's castle, the mid-17th-century chapel of Nossa Senhora da Conceição possesses three impressive elements: a heavily gilded baroque altar, floor-to-ceiling *azulejos* and a whitewashed stucco ceiling. During excavations, an Islamic door dating from the 3rd century was uncovered under the floor, where it now remains, protected by glass. (Rua Dom Paio Peres Correia; 9am-6pm Mon-Fri, to 2pm Sat)

Loulé street, with Castelo São Clemente

Museu Municipal
MUSEUM

3 MAP P74, E2

Loulé's restored castle is the setting for its municipal museum. The archaeology section's *homo erectus* kicks things off, and via dusty collections of pottery and bone you'll arrive at the Roman and Islamic periods. Medieval house ruins can be viewed under a glass floor, and the admission fee includes entry to a stretch of square-towered castle walls and the **Cozinha Tradicional Algarvia**, a recreation of a traditional Algarve kitchen, featuring a hearth, archaic implements and burnished copper. (Castelo; 289 400 885; www.museudeloule.pt; Rua Dom Paio Peres Correia 17; €1.62; 10am-6pm Tue-Fri, to 4.30pm Sat Jun-Sep, 9.30am-5.30pm Tue-Fri, 9.30am-4pm Sat Oct-May)

Praia da Falésia
BEACH

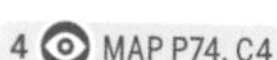
4 MAP P74, C4

One of the Algarve's most impressive beaches is this 6km-long strip of sand backed by stunning cliffs in several shades of ochre. Starting 8.5km east of Albufeira, the strand gets very crowded in summer, especially when the tide is in, but in low season it's all yours.

Praia da Galé
BEACH

5 MAP P74, A2

Beginning 9km west of Albufeira, Praia da Galé is long (5km), sandy and less crowded than many other beaches in the area.

Museu de Arte Sacra
MUSEUM

6 MAP P74, A3

This tiny museum is housed in Albufeira's beautifully restored 18th-century Chapel of San Sebastian and exhibits sacred art from surrounding churches that survived the 1755 earthquake. The main draws are the gilded wooden altar and the old *azulejos* along the walls. (Praça Miguel Bombarda 9; €2; 10.30am-4.30pm & 8-11pm Jul & Aug, 10.30am-4.30pm Sep-Jun)

Museu Municipal de Arqueologia
MUSEUM

7 MAP P74, B3

Excavated from the municipality and its surrounds (such as the castle in the village of Paderne), pieces dating from the prehistoric era to the 16th century are showcased at this small Albufeira museum. Highlights include a beautifully complete Neolithic vase from 5000 BC and a Roman mosaic from Retorta. The upper floor hosts temporary exhibitions. (www.cm-albufeira.pt; Praça da República 1; adult/child €1/free; 9.30am-12.30pm & 1.30-5.30pm Tue, Sat & Sun, 9.30am-5.30pm Wed, 2-10pm Thu & Fri Jul & Aug, shorter hours Sep-Jun)

Dolphins Driven
CRUISE, KAYAKING

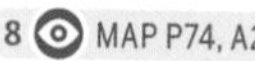
8 MAP P74, A2

Dolphins Driven runs three excellent excursions from Albufeira: a 2½-hour exploration of the local sea caves and dolphin watching;

Albufeira's Beaches

Once a scenic fishing village, Albufeira, 27km southwest of Loulé, gained popularity for its sharp, red-gold sand beaches. Today, it's devoted to mass-market tourism, particularly cheap package deals, and has all but lost the vestiges of its past. Fishing boats are now moored at the ultramodern marina southwest of the centre, and the old town – with its pretty cobblestone streets and Moorish influences – is concealed by gaudy signs, English menu boards and rowdy bars. The town's beach, **Praia do Peneco**, through the tunnel near the *turismo* (tourist office), is usually packed sardine-style with sunloungers.

Even if this isn't your sort of place, beyond the town are beautifully rugged coves and bays, though most are heavily developed and often crowded.

To the east are **Praia da Oura**, at the bottom of 'the Strip', 3km to the east, and Praia da Falésia (p76), a long beach 8.5km to the east, as well as **Balaia** and **Olhos de Água**. **Buses** (Rua Bairro dos Pescadores) serving these beaches depart from above the escalators by the old fishing quarter.

One of the best beaches to the west is peaceful Praia da Galé (p76), 9km away. Buses heading here depart from Albufeira's **main bus station** (289 580 611; Rua Paul Harris 63).

three-hour dolphin spotting off the coast; and a 2½-hour kayak trip into the local caves. (913 113 094; www.dolphins.pt; Marina de Albufeira; tours adult/child €35/20; Apr-Oct)

Aquashow — WATER PARK

9 MAP P74, A2

In Quarteira, 20km east of Albufeira, this is a huge complex with all the usual water-park attractions (wave pool, slides and sunbathing areas), roller coasters and an on-site hotel. Book online for discounted admission. (289 315 129; www.aquashowpark.com; N396, Quarteira; adult/child €29/19; 10am-6.30pm Aug, to 6pm Jul, to 5.30pm Jun & Sep, to 5pm May)

Aqualand — WATER PARK

10 MAP P74, A2

A huge corkscrew, rapids, fountains and a wave pool are among the attractions at this popular water park 15km northwest of Albufeira. The kids' area has a play castle, more fountains and mini-slides. (282 320 230; www.aqualand.pt; N125, Sítio das Areias, Alcantarilha; adult/child €29/21; 10am-6pm Jul-Sep, to 5pm Jun)

Sand Sculptures

Fiesa (☎282 317 084; www.fiesa.org; Pêra; adult/child €9.90/4.90; ⌚10am-midnight mid-Jul–mid-Sep, to 10pm Jun–mid-Jul, to 7pm Mar-May & mid-Sep–early Nov) is the world's biggest sand-sculpture contest. Artists are given 45,000 tonnes of sand to sculpt and their truly amazing creations (up to 12m high and illuminated at night) can be admired throughout the season.

It's 34km west of Loulé (13km northwest of Albufeira), just off the N125 in the inland area of Pêra.

Krazy World

WATER PARK

11 MAP P74, A2

For a diverting day away from the beach for kids, head to this animal and crocodile park, with pony rides, a petting farm with deer, goats, llamas and an aviary. It also offers minigolf and two swimming pools. It's just off the N264, 16km northwest of central Albufeira. Transport runs from Albufeira and other resorts. (☎282 574 134; www.krazyworld.com; Estrada Algoz-Messines; adult/child €17/10; ⌚10am-6.30pm Jul & Aug, to 6pm late Mar-Jun, Sep & Oct, to 5.30pm Nov-late Mar, closed most weekdays Jan & Feb)

Albufeira Riding Centre

HORSE RIDING

12 MAP P74, C3

Horse rides for all ages and abilities are available at this riding centre, including half-day rides with lunch at a local restaurant, clifftop and beach rides, plus hand-led rides for kids. It's on the road to Vilamoura, 6km northeast of Albufeira. (☎961 269 526; www.albufeiraridingcentre.com; Vale Navio 151; 30min/1hr/2hr group rides per person €20/30/50, 30min lesson €25; ⌚by reservation)

Eating

Colheita Fresca

TAPAS €

13 MAP P74, E3

Produce from Loulé's magnificent Mercado Municipal (p81) is utilised in *petiscos* (tapas) such as *ostras* (oysters) served with a squeeze of grapefruit, *chouriço assado* (flambéed chorizo) and *moelas estufadas* (garlic- and tomato-stuffed chicken gizzards), served in an arched-brick dining room and accompanied by Portuguese wines. Cash only. (☎289 070 608; www.facebook.com/colheitafresca; Rua Dr Joaquim Nunes Saraiva; tapas €3-10; ⌚9am-9pm Mon-Fri, to 10pm Sat)

Bocage

PORTUGUESE €

14 MAP P74, E2

On the corner of a quiet lane just off the main drag, this traditional, family-run restaurant serves solid plates of market-sourced grilled fish and meat in a cosy, wood-lined dining room. Get here early at lunchtime, as it fills up fast with locals. (289 412 416; www.restaurantebocage.com; Rua Bocage 14; mains €6-12; noon-3.30pm & 6.30-10pm Mon-Sat)

Vila Joya Restaurant

GASTRONOMY **€€€**

15 MAP P74, A3

Helmed by Austrian chef Dieter Koschina, this fine-dining restaurant in the Vila Joya resort was Portugal's first to gain two Michelin stars. Koschina draws on a variety of culinary influences and premium Portuguese produce to create exquisite dishes such as confit *bacalhau* with goat's-milk yoghurt and beetroot coulis, or roast goose liver with smoked eel and caviar. (289 591 795; www.vilajoya.com; Estrada da Galé; degustation menu €185; sittings 1-2pm & 7.30-8.45pm;)

Veneza

PORTUGUESE **€€**

16 MAP P74, A2

Famed for its *cataplana* – here, a delicious pork and clam combination – Veneza also turns out superb dishes such as *polvo à lagereiro* (tender octopus with baked potatoes). Its wine cellar is one of the region's finest, with over 1000 references. It's 11km north of Albufeira; you'll need a car to get here. (289 367 129; www.restauranteveneza.com; Estrada de Paderne 560A, Mem Moniz; mains €11-22; 7.30-10.30pm Wed, 12.30-3pm & 7.30-10.30pm Thu-Mon;)

Igreja de São Lourenço de Matos (p75)

Dom Carlos

PORTUGUESE €€€

17 MAP P74, C3

Higher-end restaurants tend to be out of Albufeira, but here you can splash out and still walk back to your hotel. The elegant but intimate interior, dressed in white and pale blue, feels worlds away from the frenzied centre, and the five-course menus (no à la carte) utilise market-sourced produce in intricately presented dishes. (289 541 224; Rua Alves Correia 100; 5-course menu €49; 7.15-11pm Wed-Sun Apr-Oct)

Casa da Fonte

PORTUGUESE €€

18 MAP P74, A3

In Albufeira near the tourist office, Casa da Fonte serves everything from sandwiches to charcoal-grilled fish in a beautiful courtyard lined with *azulejos* and set around a lemon tree. Staff are friendly, and the atmosphere is relaxed and more authentically Portuguese than at many of Albufeira's other restaurants. (289 514 578; www.restaurantebarcasadafonte.pt; Rua João de Deus 7; mains €9.50-19.50; noon-midnight)

Os Arcos

PORTUGUESE €€

19 MAP P74, B2

One of Albufeira's original tourist restaurants – it's been around since 1978 – the Arches serves no-nonsense, traditional Portuguese steaks and grilled seafood at tightly arranged dark-wood tables. The menu is more meat than fish, with fillet steak the house speciality. (289 513 460; Rua Alves Correia 25; mains €11.50-29.50; 6.30-11pm Mon-Sat)

Drinking

Café Calcinha

CAFE

20 MAP P74, E2

Loulé's oldest cafe is a replica of an old Brazilian coffee shop, opened in 1927 and virtually unchanged since, with a gorgeous art-deco interior and marble-topped tables. Live fado occasionally takes place. The statue outside depicts António Aleixo, an early-20th-century poet and a former regular of the cafe, sitting at his own bronze table. (289 415 763; www.facebook.com/cafecalcinha; Praça da República 67; 8am-11pm;)

Taberna dos Frades

WINE BAR

21 MAP P74, D2

Decorated in rustic style, with wine barrels on the pavement out front and striking cross-vaulted ceilings, this *taberna* serves Portuguese wines by the glass, a wide range of gins and local cheeses and charcuterie. It regularly hosts live fado nights, and the atmosphere is nearly always great. (Rua Condestável Dom Nuno Alvares Pereira 8; 3pm-2am Sun-Wed, 10am-2am Thu-Sat;)

Bar Marroquia

BAR

22 MAP P74, B1

Arabic-themed Bar Marroquia has an inviting interior with a fireplace

São Brás de Alportel

The quiet country town of São Brás de Alportel (SBA) is 13km east of Loulé. It lies in a valley in the olive-, carob-, fig- and almond-wooded Barrocal region, a lush limestone area between the mountains and the sea.

SBA was a hotspot in the 19th-century heyday of cork and there are still 10 prospering factories around the town, including Nova Cortiça (p55). English-speaking guides at **Algarve Rotas** (☎965 561 166; www.algarverotas.com; tours/workshops from €15/28) lead interactive cork tours that might include visiting a traditional cork factory, viewing cork stacks or planting your own cork tree.

Outbuildings at SBA's **Museu do Traje** (☎289 840 100; www.museu-sbras.com; Rua Dr José Dias Sancho 61; adult/child €2/free; ⏲10am-1pm & 2-5pm Mon-Fri, 2-5pm Sat & Sun) have a cork presentation as well as a carriage collection but the highlight is the ever-changing exhibition of local costumes (there are 15,000 in the museum store).

Constructed during Roman times, SBA's ancient road **Calçadinha de São Brás de Alportel** (Rua Calçadinha Romana) is thought to have linked Faro (Ossonoba) with Beja (Pax Julia). It was used by mules and shepherds until the 19th century. You can wander along two branches – one is 100m long, the other 500m. The interpretive centre **Centro da Calçadinha** (☎289 840 004; www.cm-sbras.pt; Rua do Matadouro 2; admission free; ⏲9.30am-1pm & 2-5.30pm Mon-Sat), can provide free guided tours on request.

and a pool table with red baize. Seasonal fruit mojitos, caipirinhas and punches served in giant glass bowls are specialities. Occasional live music spans flamenco, fado and jazz. (www.facebook.com/marroquiabar; Rua Nossa Senhora da Piedade 120; ⏲8pm-midnight Sun-Thu, to 2am Fri & Sat; 📶)

Shopping

Mercado Municipal MARKET

23 MAP P74, F3

Loulé's most impressive piece of architectural heritage is its art-nouveau market, a 1908 revivalist neo-Moorish confection with four cupolas at the four corners and features picked out in raspberry-red against cream-coloured walls. Inside you'll find a fish market, cheap cafes and local produce such as orange-blossom honey, fig 'cheese' (not cheese at all) and Cliff Richard's Algarve-produced wine. (Praça da República; ⏲6.30am-3pm Mon-Sat)

Driving Tour

Serra do Caldeirão

Beginning around 10km north of Loulé, this is a beautiful protected area of undulating hills, cork oaks and scrubland. Hiking, birdwatching, pretty hill villages and hearty mountain cuisine all abound. Easy to explore on a day trip, the region also has some wonderfully authentic guesthouses set within farmhouses if you want to stay.

Drive Facts

Start Alte

End Clareanes

Length 108km; five hours

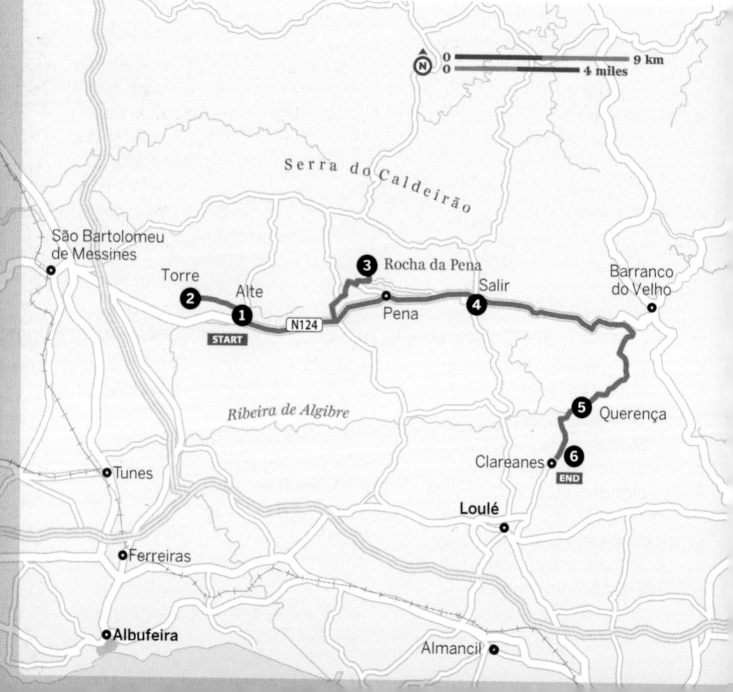

❶ Alte

Compact Alte has flower-filled streets, whitewashed buildings and several *fontes* (traditional water sources) that were used for the mills and former wells; the largest, Fonte Grande, passes through dykes, weirs and watermills. The **Pólo Museológico Cândido Guerreiro e Condes de Alte museum** (☎289 478 058; www.museudeloule.pt; Rua Condes de Alte; admission free; ⏲9am-5pm Mon-Fri) provides information.

❷ Wooden Toys

When the hamlet of Torre's school fell into disuse as there weren't enough children, three local women turned it into the **Fábrica de Brinquedos** (www.projectotasa.com/project/artisans/da-torre; Rua de Torre, Torre, Fonte Santa; ⏲9am-1pm Mon-Fri) workshop where they make charming wooden toys such as cars, spinning tops and puzzles from carob, almond, gorse and olive wood.

❸ Rocha da Pena

The Serra do Caldeirão's most worthwhile short walk is climbing this 479m-high **limestone rock** (www.walkalgarve.com; Rua de Rocha da Pena) via a well-signposted 4.7km circuit (allow two to three hours return). Local museums stock a basic map-guide. Carry water and snacks, and heed seasonal forest fire warnings.

❹ Salir

Whitewashed Salir spreads over two hills below the 12th-century ruins of its castle. The **Pólo Museológico de Salir** (☎289 489 137; www.museudeloule.pt; Largo Pedro Dias; admission free; ⏲9am-5pm Mon-Fri) museum has a glass floor above the Moorish foundations, and displays other local archaeological finds, including Neolithic menhirs, Iron Age stelae and Roman pottery.

❺ Querença

Querença is one of the region's prettiest villages, with white-washed buildings set around a square graced by an early-16th-century church: pick up the key from the **Pólo Museológico da Água** (☎289 422 495; www.cm-loule.pt; Rua Prof Dr Manuel Viegas Guerreiro; admission free; ⏲9am-1pm & 2-5pm Mon-Fri) museum, with a model waterwheel.

❻ Local Dining

A former threshing mill's stables now house the charming rural restaurant **Monte da Eira** (☎289 438 129; www.restaurantemontedaeira.com; N396, Clareanes; mains €8-16, 2-/3-course lunch menu €14.50/17.50; ⏲12.30-2.30pm & 7-10.15pm Tue-Sat, 12.30-3pm Sun; 📶👪), with white-clothed tables, outdoor terraces, and refined rustic specialities like *estfado de javali* (wild boar stew with local herbs) and *caçarola de coelho e ameixas* (rabbit and plum casserole).

Explore

Silves & Around

Topped by a spectacular castle, Silves is one of the Algarve's prettiest towns. It's also replete with history: it was an important city in Moorish times and preserves a tightly woven medieval centre. The coast near Silves has a series of beaches with postcard-perfect rock formations – a stunning sight. The resort town of Carvoeiro retains plenty of charm and also makes a good base.

The Short List

- ***Benagil Caves (p89)*** *Kayaking into this extraordinary cave with a hole in its roof east of Carvoeiro.*
- ***Castelo (p87)*** *Exploring Silves' Moorish castle, concealing the ruins of an Almohad-era palace.*
- ***Museu Municipal de Arqueologia (p88)*** *Peeling back layers of history at the fascinating archaeological museum built around a Moorish well.*
- ***Silves Sé (p87)*** *Admiring the magnificent Gothic interior of Silves' cathedral.*
- ***Slide & Splash (p88)*** *Riding the exhilarating slides at Portugal's best water park.*

Getting There & Around

Buses leave from Silves' riverfront, with direct services to Albufeira and Portimão, which has connections to towns along the coast.

Silves' train station is 2km south of the town; you'll need to take a local bus or a taxi, as it's along a major highway. Trains serve Lagos and Faro.

Silves Map on p86

Benagil Caves (p89) NIDO HUEBL/SHUTTERSTOCK ©

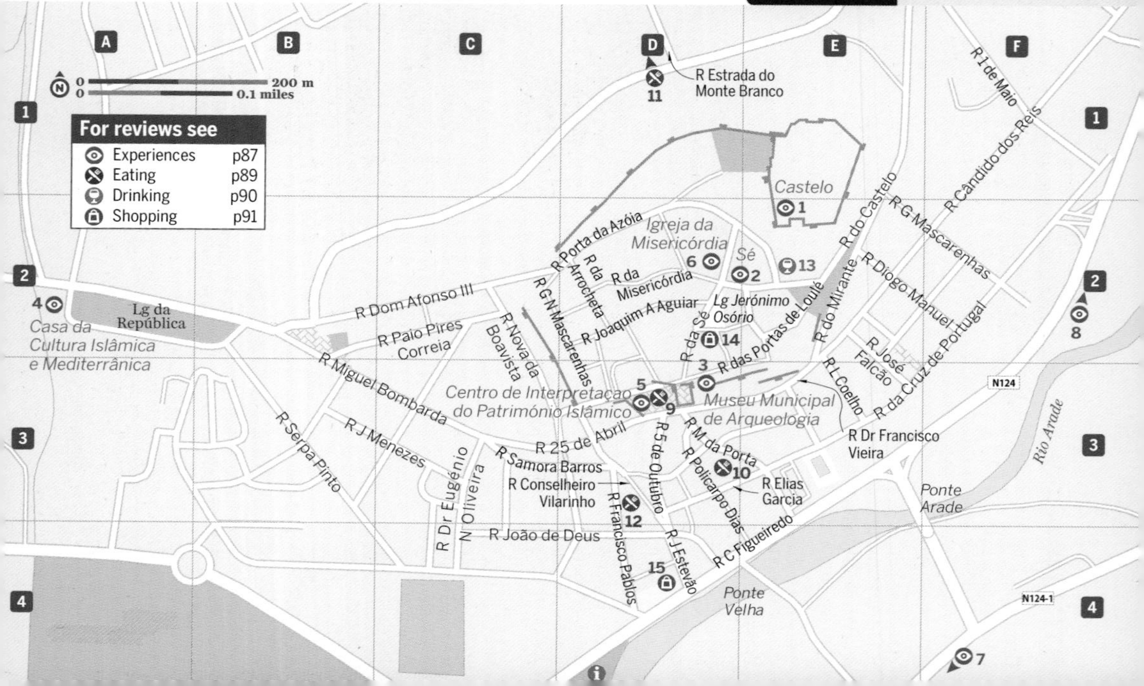

A B C D E F
1 2 3 4

0 — 200 m
0 — 0.1 miles

For reviews see

Experiences	p87
Eating	p89
Drinking	p90
Shopping	p91

R Estrada do Monte Branco
11
R 1 de Maio
R Cândido dos Reis
Castelo
1
R do Castelo
R G Mascarenhas
Igreja da Misericórdia
6
Sé
2
13
R Porta da Azóia
R da Arrocheta
R da Misericórdia
R Diogo Manuel
R Cruz de Portugal
R do Mirante
R das Portas de Loulé
Lg Jerónimo Osório
R Joaquim A Aguiar
R da Sé
14
3
R G N Mascarenhas
R Nova da Boavista
R Dom Afonso III
R Paio Pires Correia
4
Casa da Cultura Islâmica e Mediterrânica
Lg da República
R Miguel Bombarda
Centro de Interpretação do Património Islâmico
5
9
Museu Municipal de Arqueologia
R José Falcão
R L Coelho
R da Cruz de Portugal
R Dr Francisco Vieira
N124
Rio Arade
8
R 25 de Abril
R 5 de Outubro
R M da Porta
10
R Elias Garcia
R Policarpo Dias
R Samora Barros
R Conselheiro Vilarinho
R Francisco Pablos
12
R J Menezes
R Serpa Pinto
R Dr Eugénio
N Oliveira
R João de Deus
R J Estevão
15
R C Figueiredo
Ponte Arade
Ponte Velha
N124-1
7

Experiences

Castelo

CASTLE

1 MAP P86, E2

This russet-coloured, Lego-like castle – originally occupied in the Visigothic period – has great views over the town and surrounding countryside. What you see today dates mostly from the Moorish era, though the castle was heavily restored in the 20th century. Walking the parapets and admiring the vistas is the main attraction, but you can also gaze down on the excavated ruins of the Almohad-era palace. The whitewashed 12th-century water cisterns, 5m deep, now host temporary exhibitions. (☎282 440 837; www.cm-silves.pt; Rua da Cruz de Portugal; adult/child €2.80/1.40, joint ticket with Museu Municipal de Arqueologia €3.90; 9am-10pm Jul & Aug, to 8pm Sep–mid-Oct, to 7pm Jun, to 5.30pm mid-Oct–May)

Sé

CATHEDRAL

2 MAP P86, D2

Just below the castle is the *sé*, built in 1189 on the site of an earlier mosque, then rebuilt after the 1249 Reconquista and subsequently restored several times following earthquake damage. In many ways, this is the Algarve's most impressive cathedral, with a substantially unaltered Gothic interior of dramatically high, ribbed vaulted ceilings, stained glass and intricately carved tombs. The Christ sculpture, the *Senhor dos Passos*, is one of the main processional figures of the town's Easter celebrations. (Rua da Sé; by donation;

Silves Castelo

9am-12.30pm & 2-5.30pm Mon-Fri year-round, plus 9am-1pm Sat Jun-Aug)

Museu Municipal de Arqueologia MUSEUM

3 MAP P86, D3

Built tight against the defensive walls, this archaeological museum has a mix of interesting finds from the town and around. The modern building was constructed around an 18m-deep Moorish well with a spiral staircase heading into the depths that you can follow for a short stretch. Otherwise, this is another Algarve museum that starts at the prehistoric beginning but soon moves on to focus on the Almohad period of the 12th and 13th centuries. (282 444 838; www.cm-silves.pt; Rua das Portas de Loulé 14; adult/child €2.10/1.05, joint ticket with Castelo €3.90; 10am-6pm)

Casa da Cultura Islâmica e Mediterrânica CULTURAL CENTRE

4 MAP P86, A2

Built with an art-nouveau flourish in 1914, this wonderfully restored neo-Moorish cultural centre 600m west of the centre hosts occasional exhibitions, lectures and performances. (282 440 895; www.cm-silves.pt; Largo da República 31A; hours vary)

Centro de Interpretaçao do Património Islâmico VISITOR CENTRE

5 MAP P86, D3

This interpretative centre promotes the network of Islamic routes through Portugal, Spain and Morocco, with a small but interesting exhibition on architecture (including traditional mud-brick production), water and poetry. Knowledgeable overseer Miguel knows a lot about the town and its Islamic cultural heritage. The centre also doubles as Silves' municipal tourism office. (282 440 800; www.cm-silves.pt; Largo do Município; admission free; 10am-1pm & 2-5pm Mon-Fri)

Igreja da Misericórdia CHURCH

6 MAP P86, D2

The exterior of the 16th-century Igreja da Misericórdia is plain apart from its distinctive, fanciful Manueline doorway hanging well above street level (it's not the main entrance), which is decorated with curious heads, pine cones, foliage and aquatic emblems. Inside, the altarpiece has seven panels depicting the seven works of mercy. (https://diocese-algarve.pt; Rua da Sé; 9am-1pm & 2-5.30pm Mon-Fri)

Slide & Splash WATER PARK

7 MAP P86, F4

Set over 7 hectares, 8km north of Carvoeiro, this water park is widely considered Portugal's best, thanks to the sheer quantity of slides, toboggans and pools, along with reptile and birds-of-prey shows, and multiple restaurants. There's enough here to keep kids and adults entertained for most of a day, though with no family ticket available it can be an

Coastal Carvoeiro

Diminutive seaside resort Carvoeiro, 15km south of Silves, is a cluster of whitewashed buildings rising up above tawny, gold and green cliffs. Its small arc of beach, **Praia do Carvoeiro**, is the focus of the town.

One of the Algarve's most memorable walks, the clifftop **Percurso dos Sete Vales Suspensos** route connects the beaches east of Carvoeiro. Beginning at Praia Vale Centianes, 2.3km east of town, it heads 5.7km to **Praia da Marinha**, with karst rock stacks.

En route, 1.7km before arriving at Praia da Marinha, is one of the Algarve's – and Portugal's – most emblematic sights, **Benagil Caves** (Algar de Benagil; Praia de Benagil). This huge natural seaside cave has a hole in its ceiling through which streaming sunlight illuminates the sandstone and beach below. The only way to access the interior is via the water. Numerous companies along the coast, such as **Taruga Tours** (969 617 828; www.tarugatoursbenagilcaves.pt; Praia de Benagil; 30/75min boat tours €15/25, 90min kayak/SUP hire €30/60; 9.30am-6.30pm May-Sep, 10.30am-4.30pm Oct-Apr), run boat trips, and hire kayaks and SUPs (stand-up paddleboards) to paddle here yourself. Swimming to the caves is discouraged due to strong tides and currents, and high watercraft traffic. From the cliffs above, you can look down to see the hole in the cave's roof.

expensive outing. (282 340 800; www.slidesplash.com; Vale de Deus 125, Estômbar; adult/child €27/20; 10am-6.30pm Aug, to 6pm Jul & early–mid-Sep, to 5.30pm Jun, to 5pm Apr, May & mid-late Sep)

Country Riding Centre — HORSE RIDING

8 MAP P86, F2

Signposted 5km northeast of Silves, this riding centre provides lessons and rides for all levels, from one hour to multiday trips – packages including accommodation and lunches start at €990 for five nights. Pony rides for kids cost €25 for 30 minutes. (917 976 992; www.countryridingcentre.com; Rua de Pinheiro e Garrado, Pinheiro e Garrado; 1/3hr rides from €40/85, 30min private lesson €30; 9am-1pm & 3.30-7pm Mon-Sat, by appointment Sun)

Eating

Pastelaria Rosa — CAFE, PASTRIES €

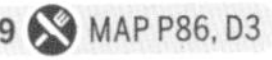

9 MAP P86, D3

Wrought-iron chairs fill the traditional blue-and-white-tiled interior and pavement terrace at this atmospheric cafe. House-baked treats include *bolos de arroz* (orange rice-flour cakes) and *folhados de maçã* (apple and almond pastries); it also serves

Rural Dining

Silves' star dining choice is converted farmhouse **Restaurante O Barradas** (282 443 308; www.obarradas.com; Palmeirinha; mains €12.50-26.50, cataplanas €45-46; 6-10pm Thu-Tue), 4.5km south of town. Sustainably sourced fish and organic meat and vegetables are used to create dishes like slow-cooked suckling pig, chargrilled octopus with sweet potato, and fava bean and chorizo stew. The owner is a winemaker, whose wares appear on the wine list alongside vintages from Portugal's finest wineries.

breakfast (fruit salad with yoghurt, cinnamon toast) and light lunches (sandwiches, salads and savoury pastries such as *rissóis de carne* with spicy minced beef). (www.darosa.pt; Largo do Município; pastries €1.50-4, dishes €3-8.50; 7.30am-10pm Mon-Sat;)

Tasca Béné

PORTUGUESE €€

10 MAP P86, D3

This rustic *tasca* (tavern), with chequer-clothed timber tables and rural paraphernalia (ploughs, saddles, saws, sickles and hunting rifles) on the walls, serves daily meat and fish specials at lunch, and an à la carte evening menu including *cataplanas* (seafood stews) for two. (282 444 767; Rua Policarpo Dias 18; weekday lunch special €7.50, mains €8.50-15, cataplanas €26; 10am-3pm & 7pm-midnight)

Recanto dos Mouros

PORTUGUESE €€

11 MAP P86, D1

As the crowds of locals attest, this farmhouse restaurant surrounded by citrus orchards is *bom preço-qualidade* (good value for money), serving hearty Algarvian dishes such as *coelho à caçador* (red wine–braised rabbit) and *javali no pote com castanhas* (wild boar with chestnuts). Views stretch south from the terrace to the castle. (282 443 240; www.recantodosmouros.com; Rua Estrada do Monte Branco; mains €9-16; noon-3pm & 6.30-11pm Thu-Tue)

Marisqueira Rui

SEAFOOD €€

12 MAP P86, D3

With a huge live tank, Silves' best seafood restaurant is a favourite with locals for its cockles, clams, crabs, Olhão oysters and whole fish, served at communal tables in a cork-lined interior. Head to the awning-shaded terrace on the laneway in summer. (282 442 682; www.marisqueirarui.pt; Rua Conselheiro Vilarinho 27; mains €14-35; noon-11pm Wed-Mon)

Drinking

Café Inglês

BAR

13 MAP P86, E2

Located below the castle entrance, Café Inglês has a wonderful, shady terrace for a

Sé (p87)

coffee or ice-cold beer (pub-style food is also available). One of the Algarve's liveliest venues north of the coast, it has an elegant interior and live jazz, fado and African music at weekends. (☎282 442 585; www.cafeingles.com.pt; Rua do Castelo 11; ⌚10am-5pm Tue & Wed, to 11.30pm Thu-Sun; 📶)

Shopping

Estudio Destra CERAMICS, JEWELLERY

14 MAP P86, D2

In a whitewashed building, Roger Metcalfe's ceramics studio specialises in panels of beautiful *azulejos* (hand-painted tiles), lamp bases, bowls, vases and more. Also here is Portuguese jeweller, Catarina Lopes, who creates stylised pieces such as earrings inspired by carob pods or bracelets reflecting almond tree leaves. (☎282 442 933; www.estudio-destra.com; Largo Jerónimo Osório; ⌚9.30am-5.30pm)

Mercado Municipal MARKET

15 MAP P86, D4

On the northern banks of the river, Silves' municipal market has stalls selling fresh fish, meats, cheeses and local farm produce. (www.cm-silves.pt; Rua José Estêvão; ⌚7am-2pm Mon-Sat)

Walking Tour

Portimão & Praia da Rocha

The Algarve's second-largest population centre, Portimão has a history dating back to the Phoenicians before it went on to become the region's fishing and canning hub in the 19th century. Though that industry has since declined, this gritty city still retains a maritime atmosphere. At its southern end stretches the broad surf beach of Praia da Rocha.

Walk Facts

Start Casa da Isabel, Portimão

End Nana's Bar, Praia da Rocha

Length 7.5km; four hours

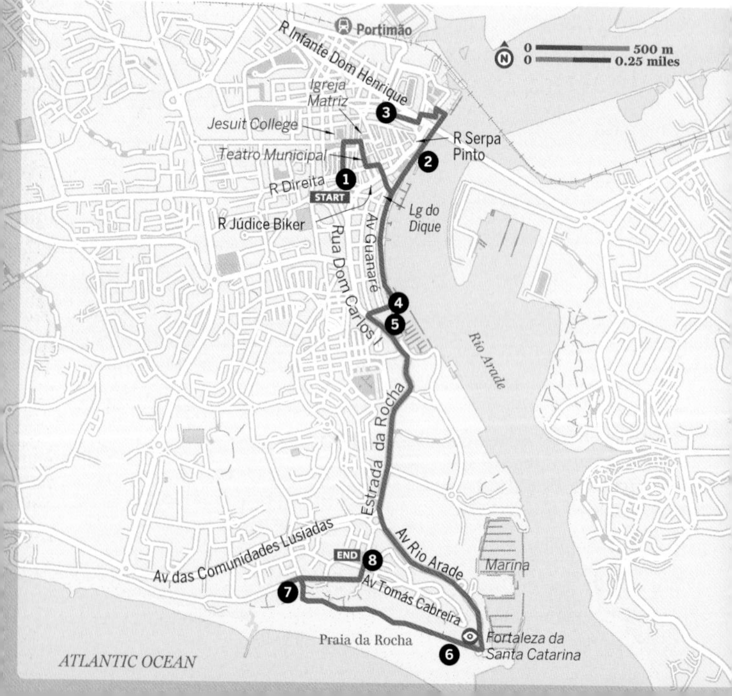

❶ Wandering the Centre

Starting at charming **Casa da Isabel** (www.acasadaisabel.com; Rua Direita 61; pastries €1.25-4; 9am-10pm;), admire handsome buildings such as the **Igreja Matriz**, which conserves a Gothic portal; the imposing **Colégio dos Jesuitas** (Jesuit college); and the **Teatro Municipal** (Municipal Theatre), which houses the tourist office.

❷ The Waterfront

Dotted with sculptures, the 1.2km-long waterfront promenade on the Rio Arade is a pleasant stroll, despite the occasionally sulphurous smell of a tidal port.

❸ Largo da Barca

The old fishers' quarter is a tight web of narrow streets near the road bridge. Just west of the bridge is a cluster of no-frills restaurants serving charcoal-grilled sardines and mackerel.

❹ Clube Naval

At Portimão's southern end, the panoramic **Clube Naval do Portimão** (282 417 529; www.clubenavaldeportimao.com; Zona Ribeirinha; mains €14-24; noon-3pm & 7-11pm Tue-Sun;) has an upstairs seafood restaurant and downstairs cafe.

❺ Museu de Portimão

This cracking modern **museum** (282 405 230; www.museudeportimao.pt; Rua Dom Carlos I; adult/child €3/free; 2.30-6pm Tue, 10am-6pm Wed-Sun Sep-Jul, 7.30-11pm Tue, 3-11pm Wed-Sun Aug), housed in a 19th-century fish cannery, focuses on archaeology, underwater finds and the recreation of the fish cannery complete with sound effects.

❻ Praia da Rocha

Drive or take a bus or taxi 3km from Portimão to Praia da Rocha (the walk between them passes the deserted port and convent ruins). Backed by ochre-red cliffs, this broad, sweeping beach is home to a marina, and the petite **Fortaleza da Santa Catarina** (Avenida Tomás Cabreira), built in 1621 to stop pirates and invaders from sailing up the Rio Arade.

❼ Ocean Dining

F Restaurante (919 115 512; www.facebook.com/restaurantef; Avenida Tomás Cabreira; mains €15-22; 2.30-10.30pm Mar-Dec;) has sublime Praia da Rocha views and contemporary Portuguese dishes such as mackerel ceviche with tiger milk (a citrus marinade) and sweet potato, and a rare *cataplana* (seafood stew) for one, rather than two diners.

❽ Nightlife

Tourist-oriented bars, nightclubs and a casino pack the Praia da Rocha strip; for a more local scene, head to typically Portuguese **Nana's Bar** (Estrada da Rocha; noon-4am;).

Explore Monchique & Around

High above the coast, in the forested Serra de Monchique mountain range, Monchique makes a scenic base, with excellent walking, biking and canoeing. The popular spa resort of Caldas de Monchique, 6km to the south, has been frequented for over two millennia.

The Short List

- ***Via Algarviana (p96)*** *Hiking the most spectacular sections of this long-distance hiking trail around Monchique.*
- ***Termas de Monchique Spa (p101)*** *Soaking in the thermal waters of this spa or indulging in a treatment.*
- ***Jardim das Oliveiras (p101)*** *Dining at this enchanting rural restaurant set amid olive groves.*
- ***Fóia (p99)*** *Driving to the summit of the Algarve's highest peak.*
- ***Igreja Matriz (p99)*** *Admiring the star-shaped Manueline porch of this church in Monchique's centre.*

Getting There & Around

Frota-Azul (www.frotazul-algarve.pt) buses run to/from Portimão via Caldas de Monchique.

Monchique Map on p98

Spring water from Caldas de Monchique (101) SOPOTNICKI/SHUTTERSTOCK ©

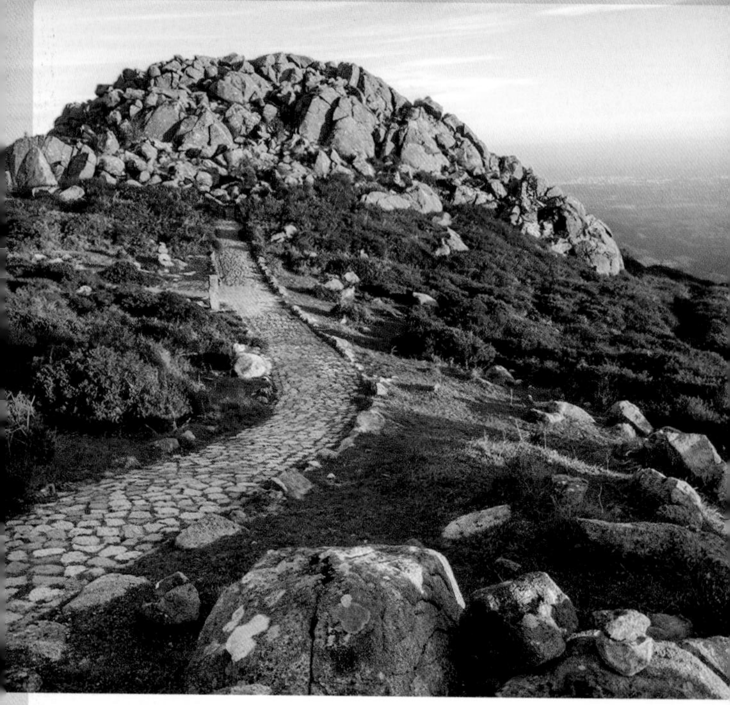

Top Experience

Via Algarviana

If you like a walk, the best way of appreciating the magnificent landscapes of the inland Algarve is to hike sections (or all) of this 300km trail that crosses the region from northeast to southwest. Some of the most beautiful sections are around Monchique, where splendid vistas open up as you climb through cork groves to the Algarve's highest hilltops.

MAP P98

www.viaalgarviana.org

Silves to Monchique

One of the Algarve's most satisfying day walks is this 28.6km section from historic Silves into the hilly interior and up 774m-high Picota, the region's second-highest point. Great views are on offer, and the terrain of eucalyptus plantations and cork forest is picturesque throughout. It's a decent workout though, and you'll deserve a hearty meal once you reach Monchique. No shops en route.

Monchique to Fóia

The climb to Fóia (p99) is an Algarve rite of passage. Though no Everest at 902m, it offers magnificent perspectives over the whole southwestern coast. It's a steady rather than tough climb, emerging from eucalyptus groves into more-exposed hill scenery. From the top you can head on to the verdant Penedo do Buraco gorge and from there to the hill village of Marmelete.

Salir to Alte

This section joins two of the main settlements of the picturesque Serra do Caldeirão (p82) and gives a good glimpse of the landscapes and ways of rural life of this inland Algarvian region. It's an easy 16km, with some decent rural eating options along the way.

Vila do Bispo to Cabo de São Vicente

The last section of the Via Algarviana is an easy 16.6km stage taking in interesting coastal landscapes, plenty of native and migratory bird life and ending at the bleak, stunning cape that marks the end of the Algarve, Portugal and Europe. It's a fitting finish to the trail. There's an alternative cliffside route, part of the Rota Vicentina (p140).

★ Top Tips

- You can download route information at www.viaalgarviana.org; grabbing the GPS points off the website can be a big help.
- The trail is reasonably well signposted, but there are some places where confusion is possible, particularly when crossing roads.
- The Algarve's summer heat means that early starts make for more comfortable walking.
- The best two-day taster of the trail is to stay in Monchique, walk up to Picota and back one day, and up to Fóia and back the next.

Take a Break

Most sections of the trail have villages at pretty regular intervals, but make sure you're stocked up with snacks and water.

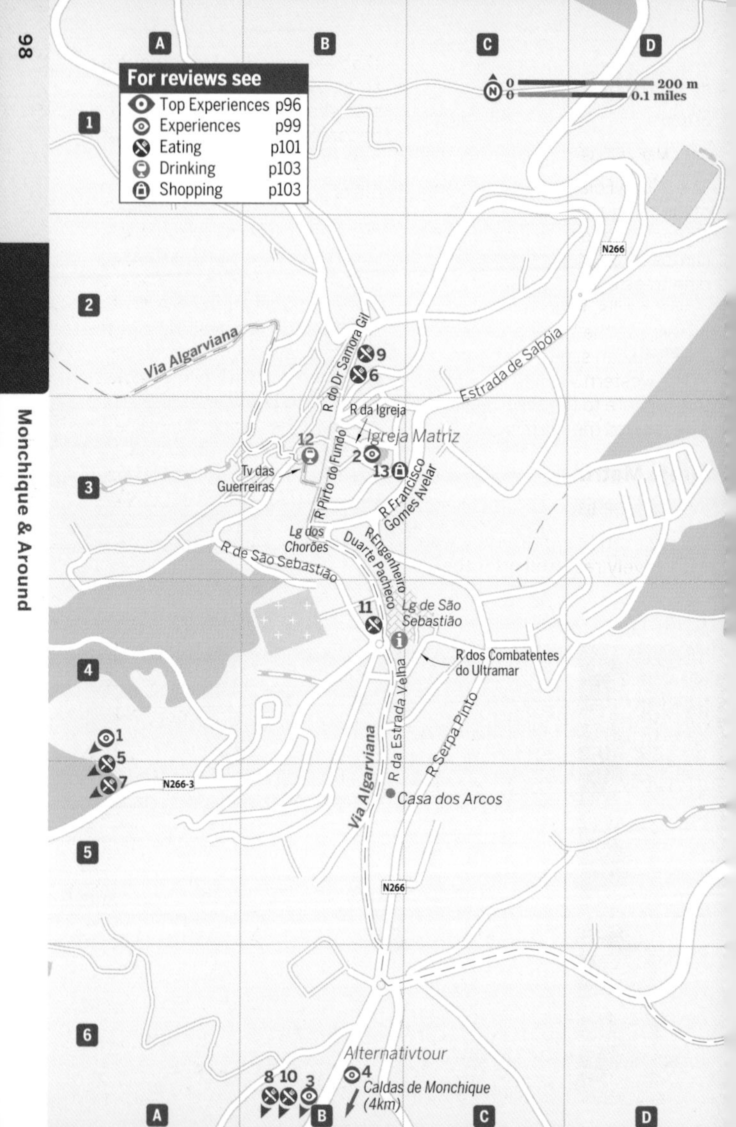

For reviews see
Top Experiences p96
Experiences p99
Eating p101
Drinking p103
Shopping p103
A
B
C
D
1
2
3
4
5
6
0 200 m
0 0.1 miles
N266
Via Algarviana
R do Dr Samora Gil
9
6
Estrada de Sabóia
R da Igreja
Igreja Matriz
12
R Pirto do Fundo
2
13
Tv das Guerreiras
R Francisco Gomes Avelar
Lg dos Chorões
R Engenheiro Duarte Pacheco
R de São Sebastião
11
Lg de São Sebastião
R dos Combatentes do Ultramar
R Serpa Pinto
R da Estrada Velha
Via Algarviana
1
5
7
N266-3
Casa dos Arcos
N266
Alternativtour
4
8
10
3
Caldas de Monchique (4km)

Experiences

Fóia

MOUNTAIN

1 MAP P98, A4

The 902m Fóia peak, 5.5km west of Monchique, is the Algarve's highest. The road to the summit climbs through eucalyptus and pine trees and opens up views over the hills. Telecommunication towers top the summit. On clear days you can see to the corners of the western Algarve – Cabo de São Vicente to the southwest and Odeceixe to the northwest.

Igreja Matriz

CHURCH

2 MAP P98, B3

Dating from the 15th century and extensively restored after the 1755 earthquake, Monchique's church has an extraordinary, star-shaped Manueline porch decorated with twisted columns that resemble knotted rope. Inside you'll find a simple interior, with a barrel-vaulted timber ceiling, and a side chapel that contains beautiful 17th-century glazed tiles showing St Francis, sinners in hell and St Michael roughing up the devil. The basement houses a small museum of sacred art, with choir books, carved statues and a tabernacle. (www.diocese-algarve.pt; Rua da Igreja; church free, museum €1; church 8.30am-5pm Mon-Sat, museum religious holidays only)

Igreja Matriz

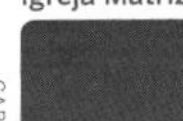

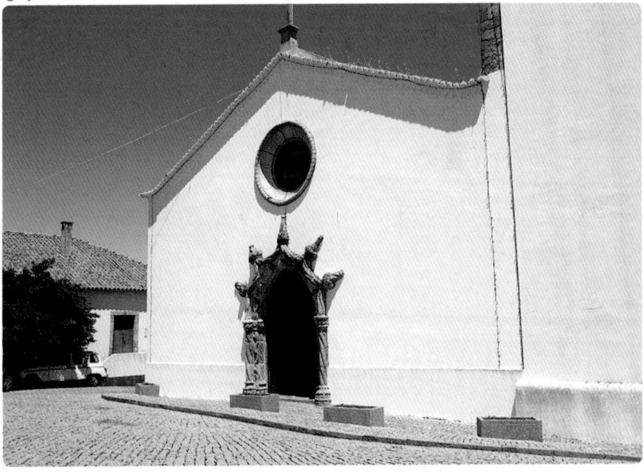

Wildlife of the Algarve

With five special protection areas (a birding initiative), eight special areas of conservation, two natural parks and one natural reserve – not to forget its sea life – the Algarve is one of the most flora- and fauna-rich regions of the country.

Rare species include the purple gallinule (aka the western swamp-hen or sultana bird), a large violet-blue water creature with a red bill and legs that nests at the western end of the Parque Natural da Ria Formosa (p38), and the Mediterranean chameleon (the only one found in Europe), a 20cm- to 35cm-long reptile with independently moving eyes, a tongue longer than its body and skin that mimics its environment. Your best chance of seeing this shy creature is on spring mornings in the Quinta Marim area of the Parque Natural da Ria Formosa or in Monte Gordo's conifer woods, now a protected habitat for the species.

Bird-lovers should consider a trip to the Serra do Caldeirão foothills. The dramatic Rocha da Pena (p83), a 479m-high limestone outcrop, is a classified site because of its rich flora and fauna. Orchids, narcissi and native cistus cover the slopes, where red foxes and Egyptian mongooses are common. Among many bird species seen here are the huge eagle owl, the Bonelli's eagle (pictured) and the buzzard.

Termas de Monchique Spa

SPA

3 MAP P98, B6

In the wooded valley below Caldas de Monchique is the famed Termas de Monchique Spa. Admission allows access to the sauna, steam bath, swimming pool with hydro-massage jets, and the thermal spa, whose alkaline waters are rich in fluoride and bicarbonate. You can then indulge in beauty treatments, from a purifying facial to a hot-stone massage in an outdoor cabana. (282 910 910; www.monchiquetermas.com; Rua de Caldas de Monchique; adult/hotel guest €20/15, treatments from €20; mid-Feb–Dec)

Alternativtour

OUTDOORS

4 MAP P98, B6

Alternativtour runs guided walks, mountain-biking tours, canoeing trips and combined mountain-biking and canoeing trips. Tours require a minimum of two people; per-person prices decrease the larger the group gets. Bike hire costs €20 per day. (965 004 337; www.alternativtour.com; Sítio das Relvinhas; tours €50-75)

Eating

Jardim das Oliveiras

PORTUGUESE €€

5 MAP P98, A5

High up in the hills, this local secret has dining rooms with crackling open fires, farming implements and black-and-white photos, and a magical garden with tables amid the olive and cork trees. Daily specials cooked in the wood-fired oven or over coals might include *cabrito assado* (roast baby goat), *ensopado de borrego* (lamb stew) or *pezinhos de porco* (pigs' trotters). (913 081 349; www.jardimdasoliveiras.com; Sitio do Porto Escuro; mains €12-18; noon-3.30pm & 6.30-9.30pm Mon & Wed-Sat, 12.30-3.30pm Sun;)

Local Cuisine

Local specialities include *presunto* (smoked ham), *morcela* (blood sausage) and *chouriço* (chorizo). On the road to Fóia, many restaurants serve excellent piri-piri chicken.

Óchálá

CAFE €

6 MAP P98, B2

Light and bright, with red-and-white tiled floors, a timber bar and local art for sale on the walls, this cafe is a great weekday stop for soups, quiches and sandwiches. It also serves traditional cakes and pastries such as *malassadas* (deep-fried dough balls rolled in sugar and cinnamon) and a *bolo xadrez* (chessboard chocolate-and-vanilla sponge iced in chocolate). (Rua do Dr Samora Gil 12; dishes €1.50-7; 10am-6pm Mon-Fri;)

O Luar da Fóia PORTUGUESE €€

7 MAP P98, A5

Perched on the cliff edge with expansive views from the glassed-in dining room and wraparound terrace, this rustic restaurant serves traditional Portuguese dishes utilising local produce: chicken piri-piri, suckling pig, wild boar with chestnuts, mushrooms stewed in port and Monchique honey, and hare with chickpeas, with excellent-value wines. It's 1km southwest of Monchique on the road to Fóia. Book ahead. (282 911 149; www.facebook.com/LuarDaFoia; Estrada da Fóia; mains €13.50-20; 10am-11pm Tue-Sun)

Café Império PORTUGUESE €

8 MAP P98, B6

Locals adore this place in Caldas de Monchique for what's considered the best piri-piri chicken in the region (ask for extra sauce if you like it hot). While you tuck in, enjoy the lovely views of the valley. (282 912 290; Largo dos Chorões; mains €6-14; 12.30-3pm & 6-9.30pm Wed-Mon;)

A Charrete PORTUGUESE €€

9 MAP P98, B2

At this likeably old-fashioned, rustic place, with floor-to-ceiling timber cabinets filled with local pottery, regional dishes include the house speciality *caldo verde* (cabbage and spicy sausage stew) and *arroz doce* (vanilla rice pudding with cinnamon). Wines are sourced from the neighbouring Alentejo. (282 912 142; Rua do Dr Samora Gil 34; mains €13-26; noon-3pm & 7-10pm Tue-Sat)

Restaurante 1692 PORTUGUESE €€

10 MAP P98, B6

Lunch at Restaurante 1692 is à la carte (eg lamb cutlets with minted aubergine purée and yoghurt; rosemary chicken with tomato salad), but dinner is limited to an all-inclusive buffet. You can dine in the contemporary interior or at dark-green tables on a charming tree-shaded square. Live music plays on Friday and Saturday evenings from mid-June to August. (282 910 910; www.monchiquetermas.com; Rua de Caldas de Monchique; lunch mains €12.50-24, dinner buffet €30; 12.30-3pm & 7-10pm mid-Feb–Dec;)

Restaurante O Parque PORTUGUESE €

11 MAP P98, B4

In the village centre, this locals' haunt serves down-to-earth chargrilled fish and dishes at green-clad, unsteady tables. It's popular with workers in the area when the lunch bell strikes. (Rua Engenheiro Duarte Pacheco 54; mains €6-13.50; kitchen noon-3pm & 6.30-10.30pm, bar 7am-11pm)

Medronho (arbutus) tree fruit

Local Brew: Medronho

You can find commercial brands of *medronho* (a locally made firewater) everywhere in Portugal, but the best comes from Monchique. The Serra de Monchique is thick with the raw material of *medronho* – the arbutus, or strawberry tree. Its berries are collected in late autumn, fermented and then left for months before being distilled in large copper stills in early spring. Homemade *medronho* is usually clear and drunk neat, like schnapps.

Drinking

Barlefante BAR

12 MAP P98, B3

Monchique's coolest hang-out, in converted horse stables on the side of a hill, has hot-pink arched walls, red-velvet alcoves, ornate mirrors and chandeliers, an ivy-clad interior courtyard, and outdoor tables on the narrow alley. DJs or live music acts play most evenings. Look for the irreverent tiled sign of the rear of an *elefante* (elephant) out front. (Travessa das Guerreiras 7; noon-2am Mon-Fri, 1pm-4am Sat;)

Shopping

Leonel Telo CERAMICS

13 MAP P98, B3

Watch potter Leonel at work in his atelier while you browse his bright, quality ceramics (tableware, tile friezes, lampshades, wall hangings and fish sculptures). The studio adjoins Leonel's courtyard garden, filled with plants in pots he's crafted on-site. (www.facebook.com/leonelteloatelierceramica; Rua do Corro 2; 11am-5pm)

Explore Lagos

Lagos (lah-goosh) has a huge range of activities, excellent restaurants and a pumping nightlife. This port town on the Rio Bensafrim launched many naval excursions during Portugal's Age of Discovery. Its old town's cobbled lanes and picturesque squares are enclosed by 16th-century walls and beyond are some fabulous beaches.

The Short List

- ***Bom Dia (p115)*** *Taking a cruise around Lagos' coast.*
- ***Ponta da Piedade (p111)*** *Walking or driving out to this dramatic headland for spectacular scenery.*
- ***Centro Ciênia Viva de Lagos (p111)*** *Learning about navigation techniques at this family-friendly science centre.*
- ***Meia Praia (p116)*** *Drinking, dining and lazing the days away on this sweeping beach.*
- ***Mar d'Estórias (p119)*** *Shopping for local food, drink and crafts at this specialist emporium.*

Getting There & Around

Buses serve destinations including Albufeira, Aljezur, Cabo de São Vicente, Faro, Portimão, Sagres and Seville (Spain). Local Onda bus 1 circles anticlockwise around Lagos.

Direct connections include Faro and Vila Real de Santo António.

Drivers are advised to leave their cars in one of the free signposted car parks on the outskirts of Lagos.

Lagos Map on p110

Praia do Camilo (p116)

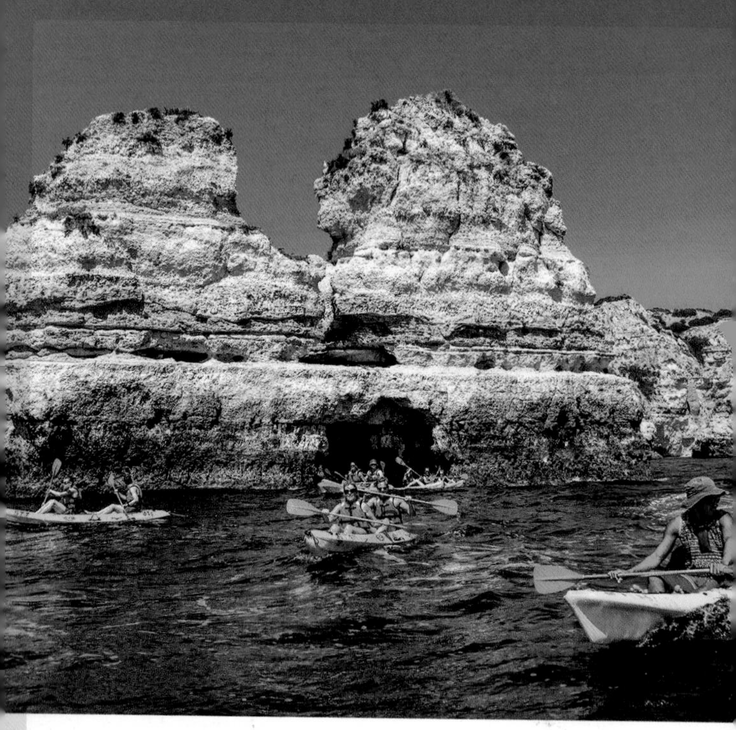

Top Experience

On the Water

Lagos' setting on a wide bay provides numerous ways to get out on the water. A huge number of companies run boat trips, which can focus on birdwatching, fishing, the striking coastal scenery or marine life. Getting active is easy, too, with water sports including diving, surfing, windsurfing, kitesurfing, kayaking, paddleboarding and more.

Dolphin Watching

A popular excursion from Lagos offered by several tour outfits. You're likely to spot common dolphins and bottlenose dolphins; Risso's dolphins, sea turtles and, occasionally, whales are also seen. (Many companies will offer a discount or a free trip the next day if you don't spot dolphins.) The trips are mostly in rigid inflatables designed to find dolphins fast, so don't expect a leisurely cruise.

Diving

The wide bay affords rewarding diving, with good rather than spectacular visibility. Expect to see rays, octopuses, colourful nudibranchs, moray eels and various crustaceans. There's an artificial reef off Alvor, which offers great fish-viewing; for expert divers, there are also some shipwrecks in the area. Several companies in Lagos provide courses, guided dives and equipment hire.

Windsurfing & Kitesurfing

The relatively calm waters of Meia Praia and regular winds make it a fine spot for windsurfing, particularly for beginners. Kiting is good here – and even more so a little way to the east, off Alvor. Several companies offer these activities with both hire and classes available. Wakeboarding and water-skiing are also available.

Coastal Scenery

Around Lagos, the limestone coast has been weathered and eroded into some fabulous scenery. A huge range of boat trips is available in Lagos to cruise along the picturesque shore, taking in various caves and grottoes, but it's even more fun to explore it yourself in a sea kayak or on a paddleboard.

★ Top Tips

- Boat trips run all year, with departures in summer from 10am until the evening.
- Most of the boat-trip operators have stalls along the waterfront strip in Lagos and also around the marina.
- Competition among boat-trip operators can be quite intense and sometimes ticket vendors will stretch the truth a bit to get you on board their vessel. Choose carefully!

✕ Take a Break

Meia Praia is dotted with appealing cafe-restaurants, so it's easy to hit the beach, eat, then head straight back to the water.

Bar Quim (p114) is a classic Portuguese beachsider. For a more upmarket seaside meal, nearby Atlântico (p114) is excellent.

Walking Tour

Navigating Lagos

The port town of Lagos has played an outsized role in global maritime history. It was here that a fleet set sail in the 15th century, commanded by Prince Henry the Navigator, launching the Portuguese Age of Discovery. This walk traces Lagos' seafaring past at its marina, museums, castle and fortress.

Walk Facts

Start Museu de Cera dos Descobrimentos

End Fortaleza da Ponta da Bandeira

Length 2.2km; three hours

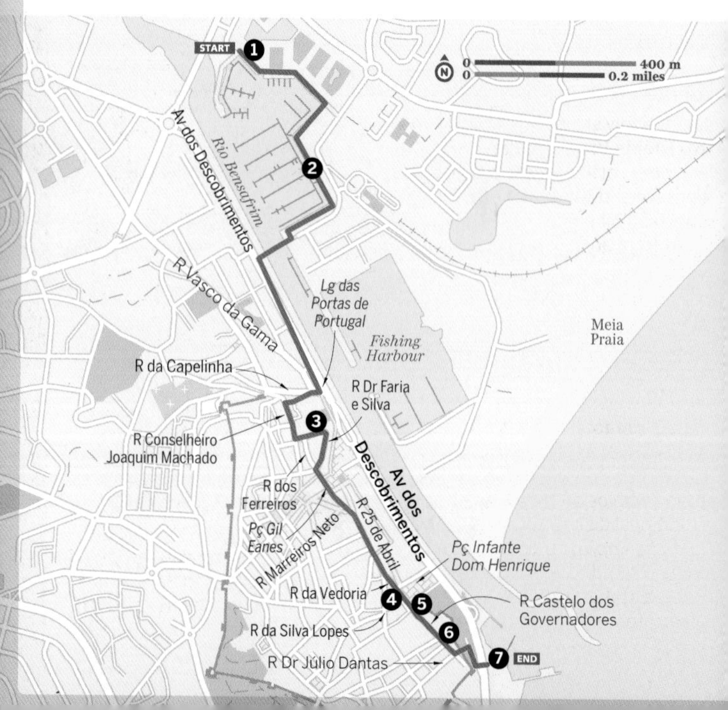

❶ History in Wax

Lagos' wax museum-with-a-difference, the **Museu de Cera dos Descobrimentos** (p112), has 22 historic wax figures representing 16 definitive points during the Age of Discovery, Prince Henry the Navigator included.

❷ Lagos Marina

To get a true feel for Lagos' connection to the water, head to the town's busy, boat-filled marina. Boat trips of all kinds depart from here, including cruises on traditional schooners with **Bom Dia** (p115).

❸ Scientific Exploration

Kid-friendly science museum **Centro Ciênia Viva de Lagos** (p111) explores Portuguese seafaring in the 15th and 16th centuries. The main exhibit explores navigation tools from ancient times to today's latest tech.

❹ Lunch Break

Stop for lunch on Praça Infante Dom Henrique, where a quaint old building houses excellent restaurant **2 Irmãos** (Travessa do Mar 2; mains €14-24, tapas €7-9, cataplanas €31-34.50; 11am-midnight;). Along with *petiscos* (tapas), it has traditional dishes such as grilled fish or *cataplanas* (seafood stew) for two. Outdoor seating overlooks a statue of Prince Henry the Navigator.

❺ Church Visit

Close to the water on Praça Infante Dom Henrique, symmetrical church **Igreja de Santa Maria** (www.paroquiasdelagos.pt; Praça Infante Dom Henrique; 9am-noon & 2-8pm Jul & Aug, to 7pm Sep-Jun) was built during the 15th and 16th centuries and retains a 16th-century entrance; the rest dates largely from the mid-19th century, when it was restored after a fire.

❻ Castle Ruins

What little remains of Lagos' **castle** (Governors Castle; Rua do Castelo dos Governadores 6) today is well preserved. Built by the Moors, it was conquered by Christian forces in the 13th century. Legend has it ill-fated, evangelical Dom Sebastião spoke to the assembled nobility from a small Manueline window, before leading them to a crushing defeat at Alcácer-Quibir (Morocco).

❼ Restored Fortress

A drawbridge leads to Lagos' little fortress, the **Fortaleza da Ponta da Bandeira** (www.cm-lagos.pt; Cais da Solaria, Avenida dos Descobrimentos; adult/child €3/1.50; 9.30am-12.30pm & 2-5pm Tue-Sun). Built in the 17th century to protect the port, it's been restored to house an exhibition on the Portuguese Age of Discovery. A beautifully tiled chapel is dedicated to Santa Barbara, often invoked as a protector against storms.

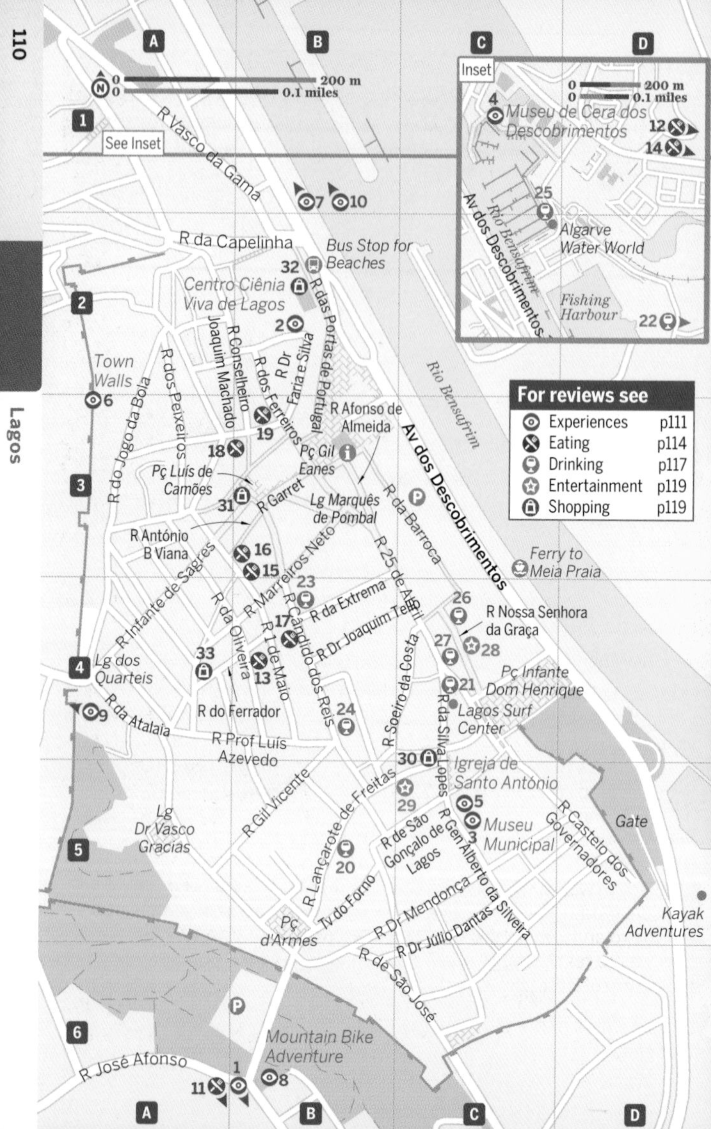
A
B
C
D
1
2
3
4
5
6
0 200 m
0 0.1 miles
See Inset
Inset
R Vasco da Gama
7
10
R da Capelinha
Bus Stop for Beaches
32
Centro Ciênia Viva de Lagos
2
R das Portas de Portugal
R Dr Faria e Silva
R dos Ferreiros
R Conselheiro Joaquim Machado
R dos Peixeiros
R do Jogo da Bola
Town Walls
6
19
18
R Afonso de Almeida
Pç Gil Eanes
Pç Luís de Camões
31
R Garret
Lg Marquês de Pombal
Av dos Descobrimentos
Rio Bensafrim
R da Barroca
R António B Viana
R Infante de Sagres
16
15
R Marreiros Neto
23
R Cândido dos Reis
R da Extrema
R 25 de Abril
R da Oliveira
17
R 1 de Maio
R Dr Joaquim Telo
13
33
Lg dos Quarteis
R do Ferrador
9
R da Atalaia
R Prof Luís Azevedo
24
R Soeiro da Costa
R da Silva Lopes
26
R Nossa Senhora da Graça
27
28
21
Pç Infante Dom Henrique
Lagos Surf Center
Ferry to Meia Praia
30
Igreja de Santo António
5
3
Museu Municipal
29
R Lançarote de Freitas
R Gil Vicente
Lg Dr Vasco Gracias
20
R de São Gonçalo de Lagos
R Gen Alberto da Silveira
R Castelo dos Governadores
Gate
Kayak Adventures
Tv do Forno
Pç d'Armes
R Dr Mendonça
R Dr Júlio Dantas
R de São José
Mountain Bike Adventure
8
R José Afonso
1
11
4
Museu de Cera dos Descobrimentos
12
14
25
Algarve Water World
Rio Bensafrim
Fishing Harbour
22
For reviews see
Experiences p111
Eating p114
Drinking p117
Entertainment p119
Shopping p119

PAWEL KAZMIERCZAK/SHUTTERSTOCK ©

Ponta da Piedade

Experiences

Ponta da Piedade VIEWPOINT

1 MAP P110, B6

Protruding 2.5km south of Lagos, Ponta da Piedade is a dramatic wedge of headland with contorted, polychrome sandstone cliffs and towers, complete with a lighthouse and, in spring, hundreds of nesting egrets, with crystal-clear turquoise water below. The surrounding area blazes with wild orchids in spring. On a clear day you can see east to Carvoeiro and west to Sagres. The only way to reach it is by car or on foot. (Point of Piety)

Centro Ciênia Viva de Lagos MUSEUM

2 MAP P110, B2

Young adventurers will especially love this science museum devoted to Portuguese seafaring in the 15th and 16th centuries. Its main exhibit covers the age of navigation from the astrolabe (an ancient instrument used to calculate latitude using the sun and stars in day and night skies) to today's GPS systems. Kids can also operate a solar-powered lighthouse, move sailboats around a pool with an air blower, use sonar and look through a periscope in a submarine. (282 770 000; www.lagos.cienciaviva.pt; Rua Dr Faria e Silva 34; adult/child €5/2.50; 10am-6pm Tue-Sun)

Museu Municipal

MUSEUM

3 MAP P110, C5

The town museum holds a bit of everything: swords and pistols, landscapes and portraits, minerals and crystals, coins, Moorish pottery, miniature furniture, Roman mosaics, African artefacts, stone tools, model boats, the original 1504 town charter and an intriguing model of an imaginary Portuguese town. Exhibits are scattered randomly through the museum, with limited explanations, making it unwittingly like a treasure hunt. The museum is also the entry point for the baroque Igreja de Santo António. (282 762 301; www.cm-lagos.com; Rua General Alberto da Silveira; adult/child €3/1.50; 9.30am-12.30pm & 2-5pm Tue-Sun)

Museu de Cera dos Descobrimentos

MUSEUM

4 MAP P110, C1

Unlike typical celebrity-filled wax museums, this one has 22 historic wax figures representing 16 different points in time during Portugal's Age of Discovery. They include Prince Henry the Navigator, Gil Eanes, Pope Alexander VI and Ferdinand Magellan (the first navigator credited with sailing across the Pacific). It's engaging for kids and adults alike; information panels are in English and Portuguese. (282 039 650; www.museuceradescobrimentos.com; Urbanizaço, Marina de Lagos; adult/child €6/4; 10am-7pm Jul & Aug, to 6pm Apr-Jun & Sep, to 5pm Oct-Mar)

Igreja de Santo António

CHURCH

5 MAP P110, C5

A baroque extravaganza, this little church bursts with gilded, carved wood and beaming cherubs. The dome and *azulejo* panels were installed during repairs after the 1755 earthquake. Enter the church from the adjacent Museu Municipal. (Rua General Alberto da Silveira; adult/child incl museum €3/1.50; 9.30am-12.30pm & 2-5pm Tue-Sun)

Town Walls

WALLS

6 MAP P110, A3

On the western side of the centre is a restored section of the stout town walls, built (atop earlier versions) during the reigns of both Manuel I and João III in the 16th century, when the walls were enlarged to the existing outline. The defensive structures extend intermittently, with at least six bastions, for about 1.5km around the central zone.

Parque Zoológico de Lagos

ZOO

7 MAP P110, B1

This zoo is a shady 3-hectare kid-pleaser, with many small primates and a children's farm housing domestic animals. There are 150 different species in all, including penguins, pygmy hippos, iguanas and snakes. It's 12km northwest of Lagos, near the village of Barão de São João. (282 680 100; www.zoolagos.com; Barão de São João; adult/

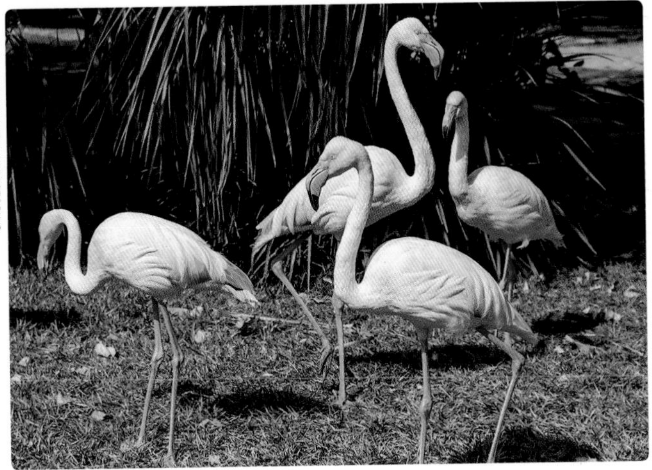

Flamingos, Parque Zoológico de Lagos

child €18/14; 10am-7pm Apr-Sep, to 5pm Oct-Mar;)

Mountain Bike Adventure MOUNTAIN BIKING

8 MAP P110, B6

Bike enthusiasts will have some fun with this company, which runs a range of outings from shorter scenic trips to mountain-to-coast trips and full-on technical rides with shoots, drops and jumps. The meeting point is on the southern side of Porta da Vila, from where buses with trailers take you up into the hilly hinterland. (918 502 663; www.themountainbikeadventure.com; Porta da Vila; half-/full-day tours from €40/80)

Tiffany's HORSE RIDING

9 MAP P110, A4

Located 8.5km west of Lagos, this riding centre runs rides from one hour through to all-day forest trips that include a picnic. Lessons lasting 90 minutes cost €75; there are also 20-minute pony rides for kids (€15). You'll need your own transport to get here. (282 697 395; www.teamtiffanys.com; Vale Grifo, Almádena; 1hr/3hr/full-day rides €33/85/140; 9am-dusk)

Outdoor Tours OUTDOORS

10 MAP P110, B1

This Dutch-run company runs downhill and off-road mountain biking (€55), kayaking (€28) and walking trips (day walks €42) between Lagos and Serra de Monchique. Departure points vary, depending on the activity. Kids must be aged 12 and above. (282 969 520; www.outdoor-tours.com; Rua Francisco Bivar 142A, Mexilhoeira Grande; tours from €28)

Eating

O Camilo

SEAFOOD €€

11 MAP P110, A6

Perched above pretty Praia do Camilo, this sophisticated restaurant is renowned for its high-quality seafood dishes. Specialities include razor clams, fried squid, lobster and oysters in season, along with grilled fish. The 40-seat dining room is light, bright and airy, and the large 28-seat terrace overlooks the ocean. Bookings are a good idea any time and essential in high season. (282 763 845; www.restaurantecamilo.pt; Praia do Camilo; mains €11.50-23.50; noon-4pm & 6-10pm Jun-Sep, to 9pm Oct-May;)

Atlântico

PORTUGUESE €€€

12 MAP P110, D1

In summer, the stunning terrace overlooking the beach is the place to be, but the wood-panelled interior with a beautiful timber bar is also wonderfully atmospheric. Both Portuguese and international dishes feature on the menu, including sizzling steaks, poultry (eg chicken Kiev) and flambéed crepes. Its wine collection has bottles as old as 1856. Kids' dishes cost €11 to €15. (282 792 086; www.atlanticorestaurante.com; Pinhal da Meia Praia L6, Meia Praia; mains €19-32; noon-3pm & 6-10pm;)

Casinha do Petisco

SEAFOOD €€

13 MAP P110, B4

Blink and you'll miss this tiny traditional restaurant. Cosy and simply decorated, it concentrates on seafood grills and shellfish dishes, including *camarão e amêijoas* (one-pot clam and prawn dish), *lulas fritas com alho* (garlic-sautéed squid) and two-person *cataplanas*. It fills to the gills in high summer, but maintains a strong local following out of season. (Rua da Oliveira 51; mains €9-17, cataplanas €32-38; noon-3pm & 6-11pm Tue-Sat Jul & Aug, 6-11pm Tue-Sat Oct-Jun)

Bar Quim

PORTUGUESE €

14 MAP P110, D1

Right on the sand, this is the best of the places to eat on Meia Praia. It's a fair stroll along the beach, but it's well worth it for the welcoming service, delicious fish soup and house-speciality spicy prawns cooked in a single pot with olive oil, garlic, coriander and chilli. (282 763 294; Quinta da Praia, Meia Praia; dishes €4.50-13; 10am-10pm daily Jul & Aug, 10am-10pm Fri-Wed May, Jun, Sep & Oct;)

Padaria Central

BAKERY €

15 MAP P110, B3

Pass through the big arched doors of Lagos' longest-serving bakery

Best Lagos Boat Trips & Water Sports Operators

Bom Dia (282 764 670; www.bomdia-boattrips.com; Marina de Lagos) Lagos' oldest boat tour operator runs trips on traditional schooners, including a five-hour barbecue cruise with a chance to swim.

Algarve Water World (Map p110, C2; 938 305 000; www.algarvewaterworld.com; Marina de Lagos; adult/child 90min tour €40/25, 75min grotto tour €15/7.50; Mar-Oct) Excellent dolphin-spotting trips on a 7.4m rigid inflatable named the *Dizzy Dolphin*. Grotto trips aboard the *Captain Nemo* take you to caves, cliffs and beaches.

Blue Ocean (964 665 667; www.blue-ocean-divers.de; Hotel Âncora Park, Estrada de Porto de Mós 837; 1/10 dives €35/270, with gear €55/450) Runs out to eight different dive sites, including reefs, wrecks and caves.

Algarve Water Sport (960 460 800; www.algarvewatersport.com; Estrada da Albarderia; water sports lessons/equipment hire per day from €55/35, 7-day surf camp incl accommodation & sports from €675) Small-group windsurfing, kite surfing, stand-up paddleboarding (SUP) and surfing lessons and equipment hire.

Kayak Adventures (Map p110, D5; 917 716 202; www.kayakadventureslagos.com; Cais da Solara, Avenida dos Descobrimentos; 2½hr kayaking trip €30; Mar-Oct) Kayaking trips from Praia da Batata give you an up-close perspective of the caves and fissures in the cliffs along the Ponta da Piedade.

Lagos Surf Center (Map p110, C4; 282 764 734; www.lagossurfcenter.com; Rua da Silva Lopes 31; 1-/3-/5-day courses €60/165/250) This surf school travels along the Algarve to locations with suitable swells.

(around since 1926) to discover an Aladdin's cave of Portuguese cakes, including *bolinhos de canela* (cinnamon buns) and savoury treats like *rissóis de camarão* (spiced prawn pastries), and good coffee. The early opening time makes this a good choice for breakfast, though seating is limited to a narrow bench. (www.padariacentral.pt; Rua 1 de Maio 29; items €0.85-4.30; 7am-8pm Mon-Fri, to 1.30pm Sat)

Mimar Café

CAFE €

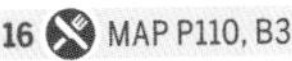

16 MAP P110, B3

One of the town's best-value casual cafes, Mimar is excellent for coffee and breakfasts (eg omelettes, croissants) and lunch dishes like toasties, burgers and steak sandwiches. By night it morphs into a tapas and wine bar serving *petiscos* such as *azeitonas* (marinated olives), *caracóis* (garlic snails), *chouriço assado* (flambéed chorizo) and *pastéis de bacalhau* (cod fritters) alongside all-Portuguese wines. (Rua António Barbosa Viana 27; tapas €2-6.50, dishes €4.50-11; 8am-midnight Mon-Sat Jun-Aug, to 10pm Sep-May;)

Café Gombá

CAFE €

Around since 1964, this traditional cafe-bakery is a local favourite for cakes and sweets including *pastéis de nata*, *bolas de berlim* (custard-filled doughnut-like pastry balls) and *pastéis de laranja* (sticky orange cake made from Algarve oranges). Pick them up to take away or dine on-site. (282 762 188; https://pastelaria-gomba.negocio.site; Rua Cândido dos Reis 56; dishes €0.80-4; 8am-7pm Mon-Sat year-round, Sun mid-Jun–mid-Sep;)

Bora Café

CAFE €

18 MAP P110, B3

Tiny Bora is the ideal place for your healthy fruit and veggie fix, with omelettes, soups, salads, sandwiches (such as beetroot, sweet potato and hummus) and delicious *batidos* (fruit shakes – try the kiwi and coconut flavour). Most dishes, though not all, are vegetarian. Tables spill out onto the cobbles. (Rua Conselheiro Joaquim Machado 17; dishes €4-8.50; 8.30am-6pm Mon-Sat;)

A Forja

PORTUGUESE €€

19 MAP P110, B3

This buzzing *adega tipica* (wine bar) pulls in the crowds with its hearty, top-quality traditional food served in a bustling environment at great prices. Daily specials are always reliable, as are simply prepared fish dishes such as grilled sole, turbot and mackerel on stainless-steel plates, and two-person *cataplanas*. (282 768 588; Rua dos Ferreiros 17; mains €8.50-22.50, cataplanas €30-35; noon-3pm & 6.30-10pm Mon-Sat)

Lagos' Beaches

Meia Praia, the vast expanse of sand east of the marina, starts 1km by foot (via a footbridge) or 2km by road from central Lagos, reachable by train year-round and by **boat** (Map p110, C3; one way €1; sunrise-sunset Jun-Oct) in summer. South of town, the beaches – **Batata**, **Pinhão**, **Dona Ana** and **Camilo**, among others – are smaller and more secluded, lapped by calm waters and punctuated with amazing grottoes, coves and towers of coloured sandstone.

Local Onda bus 2 (www.aonda.pt) links the city centre with all the surrounding beaches – the main town-centre **bus stop** (Map p110, B2) is near the market on the riverfront.

Lagos Town Walls (p112)

Drinking

The Garden

BEER GARDEN

20 MAP P110, B5

Filled with flowering hibiscus, bougainvillea and citrus trees, with a mural of a barrelling wave, this fabulous beer garden is a brilliant spot to lounge with a beer or cocktail on a sunny afternoon. The aromas of barbecuing meat and seafood will make you want to stay for a meal. Look for the kissing snails painted on the outside wall. (www.facebook.com/thegarden-lagos; Rua Lançarote de Freitas 48; bar 1pm-midnight, kitchen to 10pm May-Nov;)

Bon Vivant

BAR

21 MAP P110, C4

Spread across five levels, including two underground rooms and a roof terrace, each with its own bar, cherry-red-painted Bon Vivant shakes up great house cocktails including the signature Mr Bonvivant (jenever, absinthe, strawberry-infused Aperol and bitters). Happy hour runs from 5pm to 9pm; DJs spin nightly downstairs. (www.bonvivantbarinlagos.com; Rua 25 de Abril 105; 4pm-3.30am Mon-Thu, to 4am Fri-Sun;)

Bahia Beach Bar

BAR

22 MAP P110, D2

An essential hang-out on the sand at Meia Praia, busy Bahia has

The 1755 Quake

The huge seismic shock that hit Portugal in 1755 is usually known as the Lisbon earthquake, due to the massive damage and loss of life in the country's capital, but its epicentre was actually 200km southwest of the Algarve. The region was devastated by the approximately 8.7-magnitude quake, and what was left along the coast was battered by the ensuing tsunami. Very few buildings survive from the pre-earthquake period, and those that did weather the quake usually needed extensive reconstruction. The Algarve is, hence, very rich in baroque architecture.

homemade sangria, fruit-based cocktails, Algarve and Alentejo wines, gourmet dining (poultry pie with foie gras; lobster and cod terrine) and live music at weekends. (www.bahiabar.pt; Estrada de São Roque, Meia Praia; 10.30am-11pm daily Jul & Aug, 10.30am-7pm Tue-Sun May, Jun, Sep & Oct;)

Red Eye Bar

BAR

23 MAP P110, B4

This straight-up rock 'n' surf bar makes a top spot to kick off the night (happy hour runs from 8pm to 10pm), with a pool table, darts and fun-loving staff. (Rua Cándido dos Reis 63; 8pm-2am)

Inside Out

BAR

24 MAP P110, B4

This late opener has good DJs and a lively atmosphere, fuelled by enormous fishbowl cocktails; you'll often see people (or find yourself) dancing on the tables. (www.facebook.com/InsideoutFace; Rua Cândido dos Reis 19; 8pm-4am;)

Amuras Bar

BAR

25 MAP P110, C1

One of half a dozen bar-restaurants overlooking the marina and the town beyond, this breezy spot is especially popular for a sundowner in its interior framed by floor-to-ceiling glass or on its terrace to catch the sunset. Live music plays most nights in summer and from Thursday to Sunday the rest of the year. (Passeio dos Descobrimentos, Marina de Lagos; 10am-3am;)

Grand Café

CLUB

26 MAP P110, C4

This classy place has three bars, nightly DJs and lots of gold leaf, kitsch, red velvet and cherubs. Given its central location, it's a popular spot to end up. (Rua da Senhora da Graça 2; 10pm-6am Jun-Oct, to 4am Nov-May;)

Eddie's Bar

BAR

27 MAP P110, C4

A good-natured and buzzing dive bar, this dark-wood place gathers plenty of surfers and backpackers, who spill out onto the street-side tables. Live music (mainly rock) plays on weekends. (Rua 25 de Abril 97; noon-2am)

Entertainment

Stevie Ray's

JAZZ, BLUES

28 MAP P110, C4

This intimate, two-level, candlelit joint is the best live-music bar in town, with blues, jazz and occasional rock acts. Admission is free, but a €5 minimum spend on drinks is required. (914 923 885; Rua da Senhora da Graça 9; 9pm-6am;)

Centro Cultural

PERFORMING ARTS

29 MAP P110, C4

Lagos' main venue for performances stages everything from choirs and live music gigs to theatre, opera, comedy and dance, and also hosts contemporary-art exhibitions. (282 770 450; www.facebook.com/CentroCulturaldeLagos; Rua Lançarote de Freitas 7; 3-11pm Wed-Sat Jul & Aug, 10am-6pm Tue-Sat Sep-Jun;)

Shopping

Mar d'Estórias

CONCEPT STORE

30 MAP P110, C4

Portuguese handicrafts at this artisan emporium include ceramics, blankets, scarves and bags, along with stationery, cookbooks and music, while gourmet goods span olive oils, honey, cheeses, preserves, tinned fish, sweets, beers, wines and liqueurs. On the mezzanine, the in-house cafe serves *petiscos* and platters, as well as full meals; you can also dine on its panoramic roof terrace. (www.mardestorias.com; Rua Silva Lopes 30; 10am-7pm Mon, 10am-10pm Wed-Sat)

Loja Obrigado

ARTS & CRAFTS

31 MAP P110, B3

Inside a landmark building covered in textured palm-green tiles, this little shop sells local crafts including ceramic bowls, vases, tiles, wall hangings and adorable wooden toys and games made by the Fábrica de Brinquedos (p83) workshop in the Serra do Caldeirão hills. (www.facebook.com/loja.obrigado; Praça Luís de Camões 3; 10am-7pm Mon-Sat)

Mercado Municipal

MARKET

32 MAP P110, B2

Lagos' covered market is an intriguing place to wander, and a great spot to stock up on fresh produce and super-fresh seafood. (www.cm-lagos.pt; Avenida dos Descobrimentos; 8am-2pm Mon-Sat)

Owl Story

BOOKS

33 MAP P110, A4

Run by a friendly British couple, Owl Story has an excellent supply of secondhand books in English. (917 414 386; Rua Marreiros Neto 67; 10am-5.30pm Mon-Fri, to 2pm Sat)

Explore Sagres & Around

Overlooking some of the Algarve's most dramatic scenery, the small, elongated village of Sagres has an end-of-the-world feel with its sea-carved cliffs strung with wind-whipped fortresses. Sagres' port remains a centre for boat building and lobster fishing and its busy marina runs boat trips. Outside town are splendid beaches and the striking cliffs of Cabo de São Vicente.

The Short List

- ***Fortaleza de Sagres (p122)*** *Exploring Sagres' vast clifftop fortress.*
- ***Cabo de São Vicente (p124)*** *Catching a vivid sunset at continental Europe's most southwesterly point.*
- ***Mar Ilimitado (p127)*** *Spotting dolphins, turtles, sharks and more on ecoconscious boat trips led by marine biologists.*
- ***Praia do Martinhal (p127)*** *Strolling out to this pretty beach just outside Sagres.*
- ***Walkin'Sagres (p127)*** *Learning about Sagres' history on these captivating walking tours.*

Getting There & Around

Buses travel to/from Lagos via Vila do Bispo and Salema. There are weekday services to Cabo de São Vicente.

Sagres Map on p126

Fortazela de Sagres (p122) DANIEL MAJAK/SHUTTERSTOCK ©

Top Sight

Fortaleza de Sagres

Muscular and seriously imposing from outside, this functional fortress occupies a large, mostly bare promontory, with breathtaking views over the sheer cliffs and along the coast to Cabo de São Vicente. According to legend, this is where Prince Henry the Navigator established his navigation school. Most memorable of all is the spectacular walk around the headland.

MAP P126, B3

282 620 142

www.monumentosdoalgarve.pt

adult/child €3/1.50

9.30am-8pm May-Sep, to 5.30pm Oct-Apr

The Bastions

Most of what you see today dates from a late-18th-century rebuilding of an earlier fort. Enter via the Porta da Praça, which formerly had a moat and drawbridge; on either side, the chunky Santo António and Santa Bárbara bastions allowed for a powerful crossfire.

Rosa dos Ventos

Inside the gate is a huge, curious stone pattern (pictured) that measures 43m in diameter, which was excavated in 1919. Named the *rosa dos ventos* (literally a 'pictorial representation of a compass'), this strange paving is believed to be a mariner's compass or a sundial of sorts. The paving may date from Prince Henry's time, but is more likely to be from the 16th century.

Igreja de Nossa Senhora da Graça

The small whitewashed church **Igreja de Nossa Senhora da Graça** (www.promontoriodesagres.pt; Fortaleza de Sagres; ⌚9.30am-8pm May-Sep, to 5.30pm Oct-Apr) dates from 1570 and sits within the Sagres fortress precinct. It is a simple barrel-vaulted structure with a gilded 17th-century altarpiece. The bell tower was built over the former charnel house of the cemetery.

Circuit Walk

The highlight of a visit to the fortress is the circular walk (or cycle) around the headland, with spectacular coastal views the reward. At the far end, near the **lighthouse**, don't miss the limestone crevices descending to the sea, or the labyrinth art installation by Portugal's famous sculpture architect Pancho Guedes.

Cliff Fishing

Another intriguing aspect of the headland stroll is watching locals fishing off the cliffs. Though it's not a pastime you'd want to mention to your life insurers, you'll regularly see them pulling in grouper, turbot, bream or sea bass.

★ Top Tips

- The tour buses roll in midmorning and after lunch, so get there early, at lunchtime or late to avoid the groups.
- It's a long, exposed walk around the headland, so wear sunscreen and take plenty of water.
- Pack a pair of binoculars, too; there's plenty of birdlife, and you've a chance of spotting dolphins and whales from the clifftops.

✕ Take a Break

There's a cafe onsite; otherwise bring a picnic.

One of the best-value restaurants in Sagres is back at the roundabout turn-off for the fortress. A Sagres (p132) excels in seafood and daily specials.

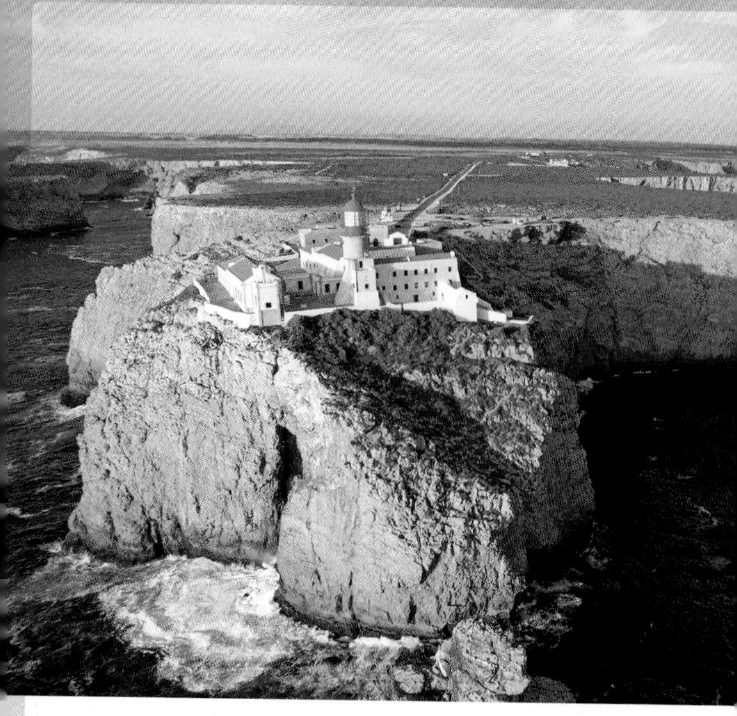

Top Sight

Cabo de São Vicente

Europe's southwesternmost point is a spectacular spot – revered even in the time of the Phoenicians. Known to the Romans as Promontorium Sacrum, the barren, thrusting headland takes its present name from a Spanish priest martyred by the Romans. The lighthouse here has a museum, but the biggest draws are the cliffs, the views out to sea and the technicolour sunsets.

MAP P126, B1

N258

Lighthouse

The buildings at the cape have had a rough time of it over the years: as if the blustery conditions weren't enough, the 16th-century convent and fortress here were trashed by Sir Francis Drake in 1587, then largely demolished by the 1755 earthquake. The current lighthouse was built in 1846; it's named Dom Fernando and has been automated since 1982. Its beacon is visible 95km out to sea.

Museum

In the lighthouse complex, this small but excellent museum gives a good overview of Portugal's maritime navigation history, displays navigational instruments and replica folios of a 1561 atlas, and gives information on the history of the lighthouse. The info is well translated into English and gives an idea of the importance of Sagres during the Age of Discovery.

Sunset

Standing here on the cliffs at the end of Europe and watching the sun set into the Atlantic Ocean is one of the Algarve's defining experiences.

Fortaleza do Beliche

Before reaching the lighthouse (1.2km to its southeast), you'll pass the **Fortaleza do Beliche** (N268), built in 1632 on the site of an older fortress. The interior, once a hotel, is off limits as the ground is unstable, but you can go through the walls to the seaward side and descend a pretty pathway down to near the water. The sheltering walls here make for a more appealing picnic spot than the wind-whipped cape.

★ Top Tips

- The area around the lighthouse can get pretty crowded with tourists, but walk a little way along the cliffs and you'll soon find a more serene end-of-Europe moment to have to yourself.
- Wonder where those ships are going? Log onto www.marinetraffic.com and find out.
- The telescopes here take €0.50 or €1 coins.

Take a Break

Snacks are available within the complex at the courtyard cafe or souvenir shop. Various fast-food trucks line up in the parking area outside.

By far the best option for a meal is to bring a picnic from Sagres, though finding a spot to shelter from the wind can be tricky.

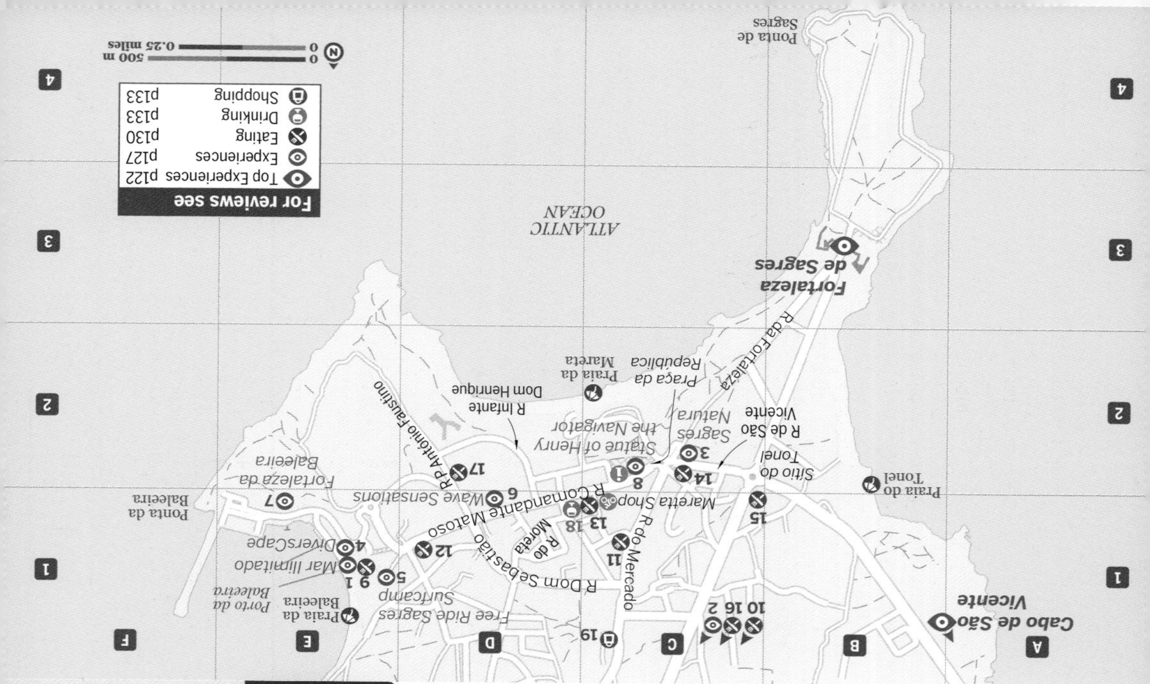

A B C D E F
1 2 3 4

Cabo de São Vicente
10 16 2
19
Free Ride Sagres Surfcamp
Praia da Baleeira
Porto da Baleeira
R Dom Sebastião
5 9 1 Mar Ilimitado
4 DiversCape
R do Mercado
11
12
R do Moreta
13 18
15
Maretta Shop
R Comandante Matoso
6 Wave Sensations
7
Ponta da Baleeira
Praia do Tonel
Sítio do Tonel
14
8
17
R P António Faustino
Fortaleza da Baleeira
3 Sagres Natura
Statue of Henry the Navigator
R de São Vicente
R Infante Dom Henrique
Praça da República
Praia da Mareta
R da Fortaleza
Fortaleza de Sagres
ATLANTIC OCEAN
Ponta de Sagres

For reviews see

Top Experiences	p122
Experiences	p127
Eating	p130
Drinking	p133
Shopping	p133

N
0 — 500 m
0 — 0.25 miles

Experiences

Mar Ilimitado

WILDLIFE, CRUISE

1 MAP P126, E1

Mar Ilimitado's team of marine biologists lead a variety of highly recommended, ecologically sound boat trips, from dolphin spotting (€35, 1½ hours) and seabird watching (€45, 2½ hours) to excursions up to Cabo de São Vicente (€25, one hour). Incredible marine life you may spot includes loggerhead turtles, basking sharks, common and bottlenose dolphins, orcas and minke and fin whales. (☎916 832 625; www.marilimitado.com; Porto da Baleeira)

Praia do Martinhal

BEACH

2 MAP P126, C1

One of the prettier beaches in the Sagres area, 2.5km northeast of the centre, Martinhal is backed by a resort development, so it's a little complex to find by car, but it's an easy 800m walk north from the port. The water is calm and the angle of entry shallow, making it ideal for families.

Sagres Natura

SURFING

3 MAP P126, C2

This highly recommended surf school runs full-day group lessons (€55 including gear) and also hires bodyboards (€15 per day), surfboards (€20) and wetsuits (€10). It has bikes for hire (€10), and the same company also runs a surf-equipment shop and hostel (dorm from €17.50). A one-week surf camp including lessons, equipment, accommodation, breakfast and a barbecue party starts at €410. (☎282 624 072; www.sagres-surfcamp.com; Rua São Vicente; Mar–mid-Dec)

Sagres' Beaches

There are four good beaches a short drive or long walk from Sagres: **Praia da Mareta**, just below the town; lovely **Praia do Martinhal** to the east; **Praia do Tonel** on the other side of the Ponta de Sagres, which is especially good for surfing; and the isolated **Praia de Beliche**, on the way to Cabo de São Vicente.

Walkin'Sagres

WALKING

Multilingual Ana Carla explains the history and other details of the surrounds on her tours. Walks head through pine forests to the cape's cliffs, and vary from shorter 7.7km options (€25, three hours) to a longer 15km walk (€40, four hours). There's also a 2.5km weekend walk for parents with young children (adult/child €15/free, 1½ hours). (☎925 545 515; www.walkinsagres.com)

Sea Xplorer Sagres

WILDLIFE, CRUISE

Leaving from the harbour in Sagres, Sea Xplorer boat trips (see 1 Map p126, E1) include dolphin watching (€35, two hours), the cliffs of Cabo São Vicente from the sea (€35, one hour) and fishing (€50 including equipment, four hours). (918 940 128; www.seaxplorersagres.com; Porto da Baleeira; tours Jun-Aug, fishing year-round)

Cape Cruiser

WILDLIFE, CRUISE

Boat trips run by Cape Cruiser (see 1 Map p126, E1) include dolphin watching (€35, 1½ hours), seabird watching (€45, 2½ hours), trips to Cabo São Vicente (€25, 1½ hours) and various fishing excursions. (919 751 175; www.capecruiser.org; Porto da Baleeira)

DiversCape

DIVING

4 MAP P126, E1

The PADI-certified DiversCape organises dives of between 12m and 30m around shipwrecks, caves and canyons. A dive and equipment costs €50/250/400 for one/six/10 dives, while the four-day PADI open-water course is €400. Beginners' courses (from €80) are available, and there are even sessions for children aged over eight (€60). (965 559 073; www.diverscape.com; Porto da Baleeira)

Statue of Prince Henry the Navigator

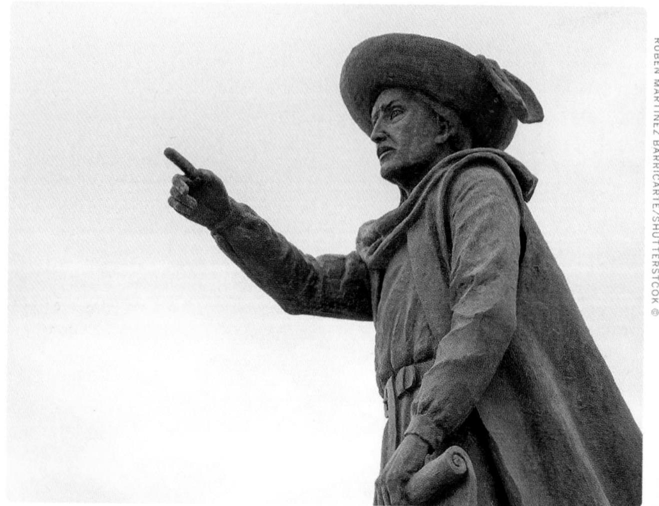

Prince Henry the Navigator

Infante Dom Henrique (1394–1460), known in English as Prince Henry the Navigator, is a towering figure in Portuguese history, and intimately connected to Lagos, Sagres and the whole Algarve.

Partly funded by his position as grand master of the Order of Christ (formerly known as the Templars), Henry built a new, fortified town and a semimonastic school of navigation that specialised in cartography, astronomy and ship design at Sagres. At least, that's according to a difficult-to-unravel blend of history and myth. Henry was, among other things, governor of the Algarve and had a residence in its primary port town, Lagos, where he had ships built and crewed, and from where most expeditions set sail. He certainly put together a kind of nautical think tank and had a house in or near Sagres, where he died in November 1460.

The expeditions commissioned by Henry advanced further into the Atlantic and down the African coast. The sea route to West Africa brought wealth to Portugal, though also marked the beginning of colonialism, as well as the European slave trade in Africa.

Attacking supply lines to the Spanish Armada in May 1587, the English privateer Sir Francis Drake captured and wrecked the fortifications around Sagres. The town was then thoroughly destroyed in the 1755 earthquake.

Free Ride Sagres Surfcamp

SURFING

5 MAP P126, E1

One of several surf schools in the area, this set-up offers lessons, packages and hire, as well as free transport from Sagres and Lagos to wherever the surf's good that day. It also runs stand-up paddle board (SUP) tours around the cliffs and beaches (€35, 1½ hours). (916 089 005; www.frsurf.com; Hotel Memmo Baleeira, Sítio da Baleeira; 1-/3-/5-day lessons €60/165/255, board or wetsuit hire per day €15)

Wave Sensations

SURFING

6 MAP P126, D1

Wave Sensations runs a range of lessons in surfing and stand-up paddleboarding (per day €55), hires equipment (surfboards/wetsuits per day €20/10) and can arrange packages including accommodation at the **Casa Azul** (282 624 856; www.casaazulsagres.com; Rua Dom Sebastião; d/apt from €110/176;) hotel. (282 624 856; www.wavesensations.com; Rua Comandante Matoso)

Cycling Around Sagres

Hire bicycles from Sagres Natura (p127) or **Maretta Shop** (Map p126, C1; 282 624 535; www.marettashop.com; Rua Comandante Matoso; per day bike hire €8-25, scooter hire €29; 10am-8pm) to pedal to the Fortaleza de Sagres, Cabo de São Vicente and the beaches.

Fortaleza da Baleeira

FORTRESS, RUINS

7 MAP P126, E1

Above the fishing port, all that remains of the tiny 16th-century Fortaleza da Baleeira is an archway and part of the walls. (www.monumentos.gov.pt; Ponta da Baleeira)

Statue of Henry the Navigator

STATUE

8 MAP P126, C2

Near the *turismo* stands this statue of Henry the Navigator, map in hand, pointing out to sea. (Rua Comandante Matoso)

Eating

A Tasca

SEAFOOD €€

9 MAP P126, E1

Seafood doesn't come fresher than at this converted fish warehouse, with a timber-decked terrace overlooking the marina and Ilhotes do Martinhal offshore. Inside, the vaulted interior's walls are inlaid with glass bottles, ceramic plates, shells and pebbles. A live tank sits alongside the bar strung with strands of dried garlic and chillies. Daily-changing platters and *cataplanas* are specialities. (282 624 177; Porto da Baleeira; mains €13-30, tapas €3.50-16, seafood platters €60-115; 12.30-3pm & 6.30-10pm Thu-Tue)

A Eira do Mel

PORTUGUESE €€

10 MAP P126, C1

A rustic former farmhouse 9km north of Sagres is the atmospheric setting for José Pinheiro's lauded slow-food cooking. Seafood is landed in Sagres, with meats, vegetables and fruit sourced from local farms. Dishes such as octopus *cataplana* with sweet potatoes, spicy piri-piri Atlantic wild shrimp, rabbit in red wine, and *javali* are accompanied by regional wines. (282 639 016; Estrada do Castelejo, Vila do Bispo; mains €11-22, cataplanas €27-35; noon-2.30pm & 7.30-10pm Tue-Sat)

Three Little Birds

CAFE €€

11 MAP P126, C1

Sagres' coolest cafe makes everything from scratch – tortillas, corn chips and brioche buns included – for its tacos, nachos and burgers (eg piri-piri chicken with bacon jam and grilled pineapple, or cod with lime aioli, avocado and cucumber salsa), all with veggie options. Drinks include 20 craft beers and gin-based cocktails. Live reggae, funk and soul plays on Saturdays in summer. (☎282 624 432; www.three-little-birds.org; Rua do Mercado; dishes €9-14; ⌚5-11pm Feb-Nov; 📶🌱)

A Grelha

PORTUGUESE €

12 MAP P126, D1

More appealing on the inside than out, with bright paper tablecloths and terrazzo floors, this simple spot is a decent bet for budget-priced grilled chicken and local fish. (☎282 624 193; Rua Comandante Matoso; mains €8-13.50; ⌚noon-3pm & 7-10pm Mon-Fri Apr-Oct)

Mum's

INTERNATIONAL €€

13 MAP P126, C1

Eclectically decorated with retro TVs and radios, toasters, bottles, books and framed photos, this cosy spot on the main drag serves mostly vegetarian dishes (such as marinated tofu with chestnut purée, roasted beetroot and wild berry sauce) and some seafood (eg cornbread-crusted cod with Parmesan foam). Staff are happy to recommend wine pairings. Cash only. (☎968 210 411; www.mums-sagres.com; Rua Comandante Matoso; mains €15-23; ⌚kitchen 7pm-midnight, bar to 2am Wed-Mon; 📶🌱)

A Casínha

PORTUGUESE €€

14 MAP P126, C2

Built on the site of the owner's grandparents' house, this cosy terracotta-and-white spot serves wonderfully authentic Portuguese cuisine, including stand-out barbecued fish, a variety of *cataplanas* (seafood stews) for two people,

Fortaleza da Baleeira

Seafood Dishes of the Algarve

Portugal's maritime history means the Algarve has a huge range of fish, often served simply grilled over smoky charcoals, with boiled potatoes and tomato salad typical accompaniments.

Many Portuguese would consider *sardinhas assadas* (grilled sardines) their national dish, and it's an inexpensive and tasty treat. Fish is often listed on menus as a price per kilo; count on around 200g to 400g for a decent-sized whole fish.

The Algarve's signature dish is the *cataplana,* named after the flying-saucer-like steel or copper pan in which it's cooked. It's often mistakenly referred to as the 'Portuguese paella', but it isn't actually very similar and doesn't usually contain rice. The pan's tight seal produces aromatic combinations of, typically, seafood and fish steamed in a wine, garlic and tomato sauce. Restaurants usually only serve it for two or more customers.

Other common dishes include seafood rices, typically served fairly liquid. *Arroz de marisco* is the standard version, but look out for *arroz de lingueirão,* with razor clams. *Açorda* is a thick soupy mixture of bread, garlic, eggs and fish (*de peixe*) or seafood (*de marisco*), while *caldeirada* is a rich broth of fish and shellfish. The unusual but typical *xarém* is an Algarvian dish of corn porridge usually containing cockles or clams.

and *arroz de polvo* (octopus rice). Its popularity means service can be slow in high summer, but the wait is invariably worth it. (917 768 917; www.facebook.com/acasinhasagres; Rua São Vicente; mains €14-22, cataplanas €28-40; 12.30-3pm & 7-10.30pm Mon-Sat Mar-Oct)

A Sagres

PORTUGUESE **€€**

15 MAP P126, C1

A Sagres' interior of beamed ceilings, *azulejos* (hand-painted tiles) and heavy timber furniture opens to a sunny dining terrace. Chargrilled fish and meats come with simple sides like boiled potatoes and tomato salads. (282 624 171; www.a-sagres.com; Ecovia do Litoral; mains €7.50-16; noon-3pm & 7-10pm Thu-Tue)

Nortada

CAFE **€€**

16 MAP P126, C1

Set on the white-sand, resort-backed Martinhal beach, this cute cobalt-blue wooden shack is a relaxing spot in the summer months, with indoor and outdoor seating. Salads, sandwiches, burgers and pastas feature on the menu alongside grilled seafood. (918 613 410; www.facebook.com/Nortadabeachbar;

Praia do Martinhal; dishes €5-18.50; 10am-10pm Apr-Oct;)

Vila Velha

INTERNATIONAL €€€

17 MAP P126, D2

In an elegant old house accessed by a lovely, mature front garden, upmarket Vila Velha offers consistently good seafood mains (go for the catch of the day), plus meat dishes such as wine-stewed rabbit, garlic- and herb-crusted lamb cutlets, and sirloin steak with wild mushroom sauce. Book ahead in high season. (282 624 788; www.vilavelha-sagres.com; Rua Patrão António Faustino; mains €12.50-29.50; 6.30pm-midnight Tue-Sun)

Drinking

Agua Salgada

BAR

One of Sagres' liveliest bars, sky-lit Agua Salgada (see 18 Map p126, D1) has a party vibe thanks to DJs and occasional live gigs. Fresh fruit forms the basis of its extensive range of cocktails (eg a 'kiwi colada'). (282 624 297; Rua Comandante Matoso; 10am-2am Sun-Wed, to 3am Thu-Sat;)

Pau de Pita

CAFE

Natural timber features throughout the rustic-chic interior of this lively cafe-bar (see 18 Map p126, D1), which has a great postsurf vibe. The upper level has a sun-drenched terrace overlooking the sea, while the ground floor has a toasty wood-burning stove and opens out to a laneway with picnic tables. Coffees, juices and smoothies are available, along with cocktails and beers. (Rua Comandante Matoso; 10am-3am;)

Dromedário

BAR

18 MAP P126, D1

Founded in 1985, Sagres' original cafe-bar is still its best, and a cool spot to hang out after a day on the waves. Spot its namesake *dromedário* (camel) painted on its facade and tiled in mosaics on its bar. Creative cocktails include watermelon-and-ginger martinis; DJs spin regularly and gourmet burgers come in veggie varieties. (282 624 219; Rua Comandante Matoso; 10am-2am Sun-Wed, to 3am Thu-Sat;)

Shopping

Mercado Municipal 25 de Abril

MARKET

19 MAP P126, C1

Sagres' municipal market has stalls selling seafood along with fruit, vegetables and meat. (www.cm-viladobispo.pt; Rua do Mercado; 8am-2pm Mon-Sat)

Explore West Coast Beaches

On the Algarve's western coast, some of Europe's finest surf beaches are backed by beautiful wild vegetation. Much of this area is protected by the Parque Natural do Sudoeste Alentejano e Costa Vicentina, an important plant habitat and home to otters, foxes, wildcats and birds. Three appealingly small towns – Odeceixe, Aljezur and Carrapateira – are the main settlements.

The Short List

- **Praia do Amado (p137)** *Surfing the exposed, left- and right-handed beach breaks here that work year-round.*
- **Rota Vicentina (p140)** *Hiking between Odeceixe and Aljezur.*
- **Burros e Artes (p140)** *Trekking with a donkey for an unforgettable Algarve experience.*
- **Kiosk Agapito (p141)** *Dining on innovative dishes overlooking Praia de Odeceixe.*

Getting There & Around

Transport links thin out on the Algarve's west coast; your own (hired) set of wheels is highly recommended.

Buses run between Aljezur and Lagos, Portimão and Carrapateira, and between Odeceixe and Lagos.

West Coast Beaches Map on p138

Hiking the Rota Vicentina (p140)

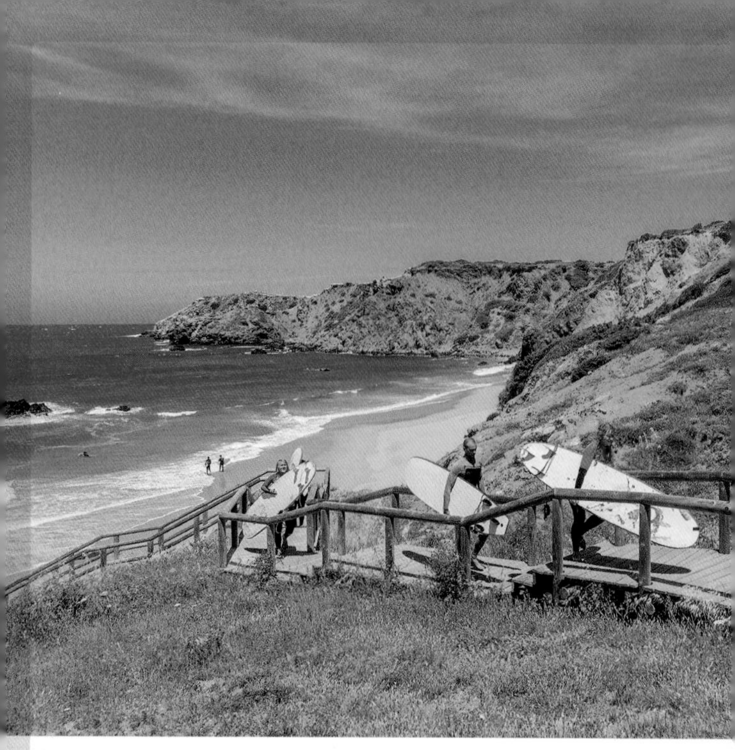

Top Experience

Surfing the West Coast

The Algarve's west coast is a world away from the packed resorts of the south. Pristine beaches offer superb beach and point breaks. When conditions are right, the mighty Atlantic rolls in huge breakers. The concentration of differently faced beaches in a comparatively small area means that, with transport, you have a great chance of finding exhilarating waves.

Carrapateira

With two excellent surf beaches, **Praia da Bordeira** (Praia Carrapateira) and **Praia do Amado** (pictured), within walking distance of town, this is a great spot to base yourself. The southern beach, Praia do Amado, offers a reliable year-round beach break and is long enough not to get overcrowded. Praia da Bordeira is also long and dependable, though beware of rocks on some entries.

Surf Schools

Most surf schools offer lessons for beginners, improvers and serious surfers, as well as accommodation packages, and board and accessory hire. Many also provide transport services to where the waves are best that day. If you want better nightlife than the west coast offers, there are several based in Sagres and Lagos, too.

Aljezur

Though there's no beach within walking distance, the charming castle-topped town of Aljezur is handily placed for many of the west's finest surf beaches, including the two waves – an easy beach break and a more notable right-hand point/reef break – utilised by surf school **Arrifana** (☎961 690 249; www.arrifanasurfschool.com; Praia da Arrifana; 1-/3-/5-day course €55/150/225, surfboard/wetsuit hire per half-day €20/10; ⏲closed Feb); the tougher, speedy right-hand point break of shingled Praia do Canal; and the steady lefts and rights of spectacular **Praia da Amoreira**.

Local Conditions

As the beaches are close together, local surfers tend to keep an eye on conditions and hit several strands in one day. The Algarve's beaches tend to be quite tidal and are usually at their best around high tide. The offshore winds that make for the best surfing are mostly easterlies or northeasterlies, depending on the orientation of the beach.

★ Top Tips

- Find out where the waves will be at Magicseaweed (www.magicseaweed.com) or the Hydrographic Institute (www.hidrografico.pt).
- The Surf School Association of Costa Vicentina (www.algarvesurfschoolsassociation.com) lists registered surf schools that follow rules and regulations set out by the organisation.
- Localism isn't a huge problem, but does exist. Be respectful and friendly.
- Theft from cars is prevalent; don't leave any valuables in vehicles at beach car parks.

✕ Take a Break

Several west coast beaches have snack bars, cafes and seasonal bar-restaurants.

Self-caterers can pick up fresh produce at Aljezur's **Mercado Municipal** (Rua 25 de Abril; ⏲8am-2pm Mon-Sat).

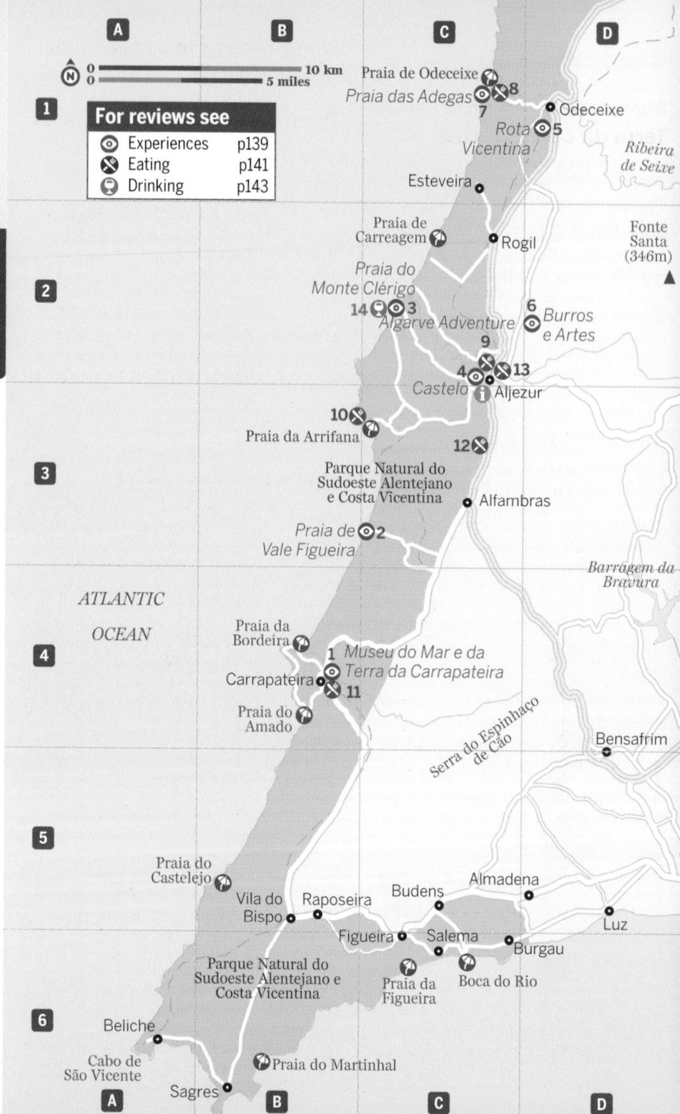

A
B
C
D
1
2
3
4
5
6
0 10 km
0 5 miles
For reviews see
Experiences p139
Eating p141
Drinking p143
Praia de Odeceixe
Praia das Adegas
7
8
Odeceixe
Rota Vicentina
5
Ribeira de Seixe
Esteveira
Praia de Carreagem
Rogil
Fonte Santa (346m)
Praia do Monte Clérigo
14
3
Algarve Adventure
6
Burros e Artes
9
4
13
Castelo
Aljezur
10
Praia da Arrifana
12
Parque Natural do Sudoeste Alentejano e Costa Vicentina
Alfambras
Praia de Vale Figueira
2
Barragem da Bravura
ATLANTIC OCEAN
Praia da Bordeira
1
Museu do Mar e da Terra da Carrapateira
Carrapateira
11
Praia do Amado
Serra do Espinhaço de Cão
Bensafrim
Praia do Castelejo
Vila do Bispo
Raposeira
Budens
Almadena
Luz
Figueira
Salema
Burgau
Parque Natural do Sudoeste Alentejano e Costa Vicentina
Praia da Figueira
Boca do Rio
Beliche
Cabo de São Vicente
Praia do Martinhal
Sagres

Experiences

Museu do Mar e da Terra da Carrapateira MUSEUM

1 MAP P138, B4

The Carrapateira Land & Sea Museum is a must for visitors – surfers or otherwise. Up a steep hill 200m east of the town square, its contemporary design space has small exhibits covering everything from the fishing industry to the daily life of locals, and intriguing photographic collages depicting the Carrapateira of yesteryear (there's minimal English labelling). The vista from the museum's viewing window over the dunes is sublime. (☎282 970 000; www.cm-aljezur.pt; Rua do Pescador, Carrapateira; adult/child €2.70/1.10; ⏰10am-noon & 1.30-4.30pm Tue-Sat Jun-Sep, 11am-6pm Tue-Sat Oct-May)

Praia de Vale Figueira BEACH

2 MAP P138, C3

One of the more remote west-coast beaches, this wide, magnificent stretch of sand has an ethereal beauty, backed by stratified cliffs hazy in the ocean spray. It's reached by a rough, partly paved road that runs some 5km from the main road at a point 10km north of Carrapateira (take the northern of the two turn-offs). There are no facilities.

Praia do Monte Clérigo BEACH

3 MAP P138, C2

One of the emblematic beaches southwest of Aljezur (8.5km from

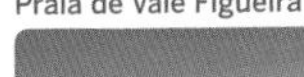

Praia de Vale Figueira

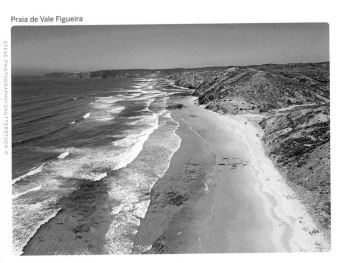

town), Monte Clérigo is a deep strip of sand with a laid-back surfer vibe. Behind it is a small village with lively bar-restaurants and low-rise holiday rental properties.

Castelo

CASTLE

4 MAP P138, C2

On the site of an Iron Age fort, the polygonal castle was built by the Moors in the 10th century, conquered by the Christians in 1249, then abandoned in the late 15th century. The walls and a couple of towers survive, as well as a cistern. Sweeping views of the surrounding area extend from the rock in its centre and ramparts. (Rua dom Paio Pires Correìa, Aljezur; admission free; 24hr)

Rota Vicentina

HIKING

5 MAP P138, D1

This 350km-long walking route enters the Algarve at Odeceixe and continues right down the west coast to Cabo de São Vicente. The day walk from Odeceixe south to Aljezur (19.5km) is an easy introduction, heading through mostly flat local farmland. It's a picturesque glimpse of Portuguese rural life. Optional detours take you right to the coast for clifftop stretches. (www.rotavicentina.com)

Burros e Artes

TOURS

6 MAP P138, D1

Fans of slow travel will enjoy covering 10km to 15km per day on foot through stunning landscapes, accompanied by your *burro* (donkey), which carries your luggage. This company coordinates trips including accommodation, food and optional multilingual guides; alternatively go it alone, in which case the added fun is tending to the donkey (there are strict rules regarding its care). (967 145 306, 282 995 068; www.burros-artes.blogspot.com; Vale das Amoreiras; self-guided donkey trek per day from €60, 1-/3-/7-day guided tours from €85/490/895)

Algarve Adventure

OUTDOORS

The energetic team at Algarve Adventure (see 3 Map p138, C2) can take you rock climbing along the coast and in the Algarve's hilly interior. Prices include transport and gear. The company also runs a local surf school (half-/full-day lesson with gear €35/60), and rents equipment (surfboard/wetsuit per day €25/10) and mountain bikes (half-/full day from €15/20). (913 533 363; www.algarve-adventure.com; Praia do Monte Clérigo; 4hr rock-climbing course beginner/advanced from €60/120)

Praia das Adegas

BEACH

7 MAP P138, C1

If you're not a fan of tan lines, head to secluded Praia das Adegas. Tucked 350m south of Praia de Odeceixe, it's one of the Algarve's four official nudist beaches, and the only one on the region's west coast. (Rua da Praia, Praia de Odeceixe)

Aljezur's Museums

Four Aljezur museums are accessible on the same ticket.

The small but likeable **Museu Municipal** (www.cm-aljezur.pt; Largo 5 de Outubro; €2.20; 9am-1pm & 2-6pm Tue-Sat Jun-Sep, to 5pm Tue-Sat Oct-May) has an archaeological collection, Islamic section and an ethnographic display spanning clocks to carts.

Built in the 16th century and damaged in the 1755 earthquake, the Igreja da Misericórdia church was reconstructed in the 18th century. Highlights of its small religious-art museum, **Museu de Arte Sacra** (www.cm-aljezur.pt; Rua dom Paio Pires Correia; €2.20; 9am-1pm & 2-6pm Tue-Sat Jun-Sep, to 5pm Tue-Sat Oct-May), include the old church bell and a 14th-century crown.

The chapel-housed **Museu Antoniano** (Rua de Santo António; €2.20; 9am-1pm & 2-6pm Tue-Sat Jun-Sep, by appointment Oct-May), devoted to St Anthony, displays paintings, books, coins and icons.

Quaint house **Casa Museu Pintor José Cercas** (Rua do Castelo; €2.20; 9am-1pm & 2-6pm Tue-Sat Jun-Sep, to 5pm Tue-Sat Oct-May) belonged to Portuguese painter José Cercas (1914–92), who left his home and collection of furniture, artworks and personal objects to the town.

Eating

Kiosk Agapito

CAFE €

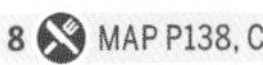

8 MAP P138, C1

Overlooking the surf, this new-generation beach cafe with aqua-and-white tiles and terrace-only seating uses local produce in breakfasts, sharing platters, open-faced toasties (like tinned mackerel, red onion, olive tapenade and sweet potato), burgers and huge salads (eg sardine and octopus). Knock back fresh juices, Portuguese-roasted coffee, beer, cider, wine, sangria or gin. Live music plays Saturdays in July and August. (926 771 356; www.agapito.pt; Rua da Praia, Praia de Odeceixe; dishes €3.50-12.50; 9am-11pm early Jan-Oct)

Mó Veggie Bistro

VEGETARIAN, VEGAN €

9 MAP P138, C2

A former wheat mill now houses this brilliant split-level bistro with raw timbers, comfy sofas and suspended lighting. All dishes are vegetarian and many are vegan. Menu highlights include Vietnamese spring rolls, sweet-potato hummus with beetroot, basil, mango and chia-seed salad, towering bean-patty burgers and open-faced toasties, plus cakes (some gluten-free). Yoga workshops and live music gigs regularly take place. (☎925 289 246; www.facebook.com/MoVeggieBistro; Rua João Dias Mendes 13, Aljezur; dishes €5.50-11; 12.30-4pm & 6.30-10pm Tue-Sat Apr-Nov;)

O Paulo

SEAFOOD €€

10 MAP P138, B3

Adjacent to the ruined fortress of Arrifana, O Paulo has a romantic covered terrace with majestic clifftop views as far as Cabo de São Vicente. The vistas are hard to live up to, but it succeeds, with tanks of live lobsters and crabs, superfresh fish and delicacies such as razor clams and traditional brine-boiled goose barnacles (a local speciality). (☎934 975 250; www.restauranteopaulo.com; Rua Serpa Pinto 32, Arrifana; mains €9-25; kitchen 9.30am-10pm, bar to midnight Apr-Nov, hours vary Nov-Mar;)

Microbar Carrapateira

CAFE €

11 MAP P138, B4

Umbrellas shade the tables at this summer cafe on the town's cobbled square. It's a lively pre- or postsurf hang-out for bruschetta, burgers, vibrant salads, coffee (soy milk available) and cake, or just an ice-cold *imperial* (small draught beer) or cocktail in the sun. (Largo do Comercio 7; dishes €6-12; 10am-10pm Jul & Aug, to 9pm Mar-Jun & Sep)

Bistrot Gulli

MEDITERRANEAN €€

12 MAP P138, C3

On the main road 4.5km south of Aljezur, what looks like a standard driver's lunch stop surprises with

Aljezur Castelo (p140)

R.NAGY/SHUTTERSTOCK ©

Best West Coast Surf Schools

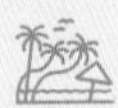

Arrifana Surf School (p137) Based at **Praia da Arrifana** (Map p138, C3), this surf school offers a complete range of hire and lessons.

Odeceixe Surf School (☎963 170 493; www.odeceixesurfschool.com; Praia de Odeceixe; 1-/3-/5-day courses €60/165/250, half-day surfboard/wetsuit hire €20/10; ⏲10.30am-7pm) This friendly **Praia de Odeceixe** (Map p138, C1) set-up will transport you to whatever local beach has the best waves that day.

Algarve Surf School (☎962 846 771; www.algarvesurfschool.com; Praia do Amado; day-long group lesson €50, week-long package from €305) Based at **Praia do Amado** (p137), Algarve Surf School runs classes for all abilities (including for kids).

Amado Surfcamp (☎927 831 568; www.amadosurfcamp.com; Praia do Amado; day-long group lesson €60, week-long package from €255) Operating out of a shack on Praia do Amado, Amado Surfcamp has day courses and various accommodation packages.

a contemporary interior, covered terrace and a garden that provides fresh herbs for salads, steaming pizzas, pastas, risottos and beef carpaccio. (☎282 994 344; www.facebook.com/gullibistrot; Sítio de Santa Susana, N120; mains €7-16; ⏲12.30-10pm daily Jun-Sep, 12.30-10pm Tue-Sun Mar-May & Oct-early Jan)

Pont'a Pé

PORTUGUESE €€

13 MAP P138, C2

With gleaming timber floors, raked beamed ceilings and an umbrella-shaded outdoor terrace, this down-to-earth place by the bridge serves daily seafood specials such as octopus with local sweet potato, grilled sardines and chorizo-stuffed squid. (☎282 998 104; www.pontape.pt; Largo da Liberdade 12; mains €9-17; ⏲10am-11pm Mon-Sat)

Drinking

O Sargo

BAR

14 MAP P138, C2

Directly across from the beach, with glass walls buffering the wind and sand, O Sargo is a great place to slake your postsurf thirst, with cold-pressed juices, craft beers, ciders, local wines, and white and red sangrias. Live music – everything from fado to Spanish flamenco and funk – plays on weekends from June to September; the bar also hosts regular full-moon parties. (☎912 995 839; Praia do Monte Clerigo; ⏲9am-10pm Thu-Tue Mar–mid-Nov)

Survival Guide

Square in Lagos (p105) ALVARO GERMAN VILELA/SHUTTERSTOCK ©

Before You Go

Book Your Stay

The Algarve has the full range of options you'd expect to find in a resort region, from surfer hostels and campgrounds to atmospheric inns and five-star properties. Rates skyrocket in July and especially August (the Portuguese holiday month), when most visitors have prebooked package accommodation and a bed can be almost impossible to come by. From September to June, you can get some serious bargains, particularly if you book ahead.

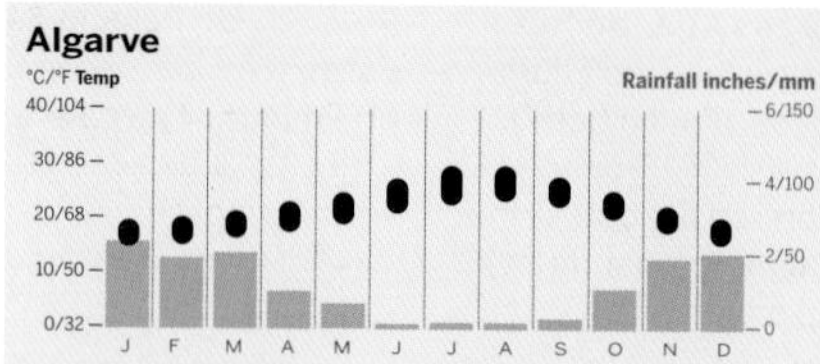

When to Go

Any time The region is blessed with good weather, with a mild winter and sunshine almost year-round.

Feb–Mar See and smell the abundance of almond and orange blossoms.

Apr–May Hike inland amid the wildflowers and leafy hillsides or get in preseason swims.

Useful Websites

Lonely Planet (www.lonelyplanet.com/portugal) Destination information, hotel bookings, traveller forum and more.

Visit Algarve (www.visitalgarve.pt) Official tourism site.

Portugal Tourism (www.visitportugal.com) Portugal's official tourism site.

Best Budget

Casa d'Alagoa (www.farohostel.com) Cool, laid-back hostel in central Faro with a sociable lounge, terrace and barbecue area.

Hospedaria Dom Fernando (www.domfernandoloule.com) Buttercup-yellow guesthouse behind Loulé's historic market.

Orbitur Sagres (www.orbitur.com) Well-maintained, pine tree–shaded campground near Cabo de São Vicente with pitches and cabins.

Old Town Lagos Hostel (www.oldtownlagoshostel.com) Good-time hostel in the heart of Lagos' old town.

Hotel Residencial Princesa do Gilão (www.hotelprincesadogilao.com) Welcoming small hotel on the river in Tavira.

Casa das Oliveiras (www.casa-das-oliveiras.com) Rural five-room B&B outside Silves.

Best Midrange

O Castelo (www.ocastelo.net) Gleamingly maintained guesthouse right on the beach at Carvoeiro.

Lagos Atlantic Hotel (www.facebook.com/lagos.atlantic.hotel) Stylish 2018-opened hotel on the outskirts of Lagos with handy lock-up parking.

Allons-y Guesthouse (☎969 870 585) Charming guesthouse with a fantastic terrace overlooking Loulé's rooftops.

B&B Candelária (www.casa-candelaria.com) Rustic Serra do Caldeirão farmhouse B&B surrounded by olive, carob and almond trees.

Casa Bamboo (https://casa-bamboo-bb.business.site) Ecofriendly, rammed-earth and wood guesthouse at Carrapateira on the surf coast.

Casa Azul (www.casaazulsagres.com) Azure-blue Sagres guesthouse with its own surf school.

Best Top End

Villa Monte (www.vilamonte.com) Stunningly designed farmhouse estate amid olive groves, orange orchards and bougainvillea-filled gardens near Olhão.

Pousada do Palácio de Estoi (www.pousadas.pt) Rococo-style palace with a coral-pink facade set in formal Versailles-style gardens in Estói.

Hotel Faro (www.hotelfaro.pt) Modern hotel on Faro's main square overlooking the marina, with a rooftop pool.

Agapito Beach House (www.agapito.pt) Brilliantly located, fully equipped self-catering apartments at Odeceixe's surf beach.

Maria Nova (www.ap-hotelsresorts.com) Contemporary Tavira hotel overlooking the grounds' free-form pool and palm-planted gardens.

Pousada do Infante (www.pousadas.pt) Upmarket inn at Sagres with magical sunset views and a floodlit swimming pool.

Arriving in the Algarve

Faro Airport

The manageable size and proximity to the town centre of **Faro Airport** (FAO; ☎289 800 800; www.aeroportofaro.pt; 📶), 7km west of town, makes arriving here a breeze.

Próximo (☎289 899 700; www.proximo.pt; Avenida da República 5) city buses 14 and 16 (€2.20, 15 minutes, up to two per hour) run to the **bus station** (☎289 899 760; Avenida da República 5). From here it's an easy stroll to the centre.

Ring 289 895 795 for a taxi or find one at the taxi ranks outside the train and bus stations, and at the airport. A taxi into town costs around €20 (20% more after 10pm and on weekends), plus around €2 for each luggage item.

Faro Train Station

Faro's train station is 500m northwest of the centre.

There are five direct trains from Lisbon daily (€22.90, four hours). You can also get to Porto (€42.40, six to eight hours, four daily), sometimes changing at Lisbon.

Regional services:

Albufeira (€3.35, 30

minutes, every two hours)

Lagos (€7.30, 1¾ hours, every two hours)

Vila Real de Santo António (€5.25, 1¼ hours, hourly) via Olhão (€1.45, 10 minutes)

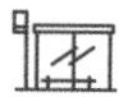

Getting Around

Bicycle

- Distances aren't great, so cycling is a good way of getting around.
- Plot your coastal routes to avoid the main roads, which can get very busy. You'll find less traffic in the hilly, but beautiful, interior.
- There are hire places in nearly every coastal town. City/mountain/electric bike hire starts at €8/13/35.
- A lot of Algarve villages have cobbled streets and wheel-chasing dogs – beware!

Bus

A good bus network runs along the Algarve coast and to Loulé. From here, you can access inland Algarve, although services become more limited. Two big bus companies, Eva (www.eva-bus.com) and Rede Expressos (www.rede-expressos.pt), zip frequently between the Algarve and elsewhere in Portugal. Smaller lines include Frota Azul (www.frotazul-algarve.pt).

Car

Most main towns have reliable car-hire outlets; companies can usually provide an electronic road-toll tag so tolls are automatically added to your rental bill. Comprehensive toll information, including a calculator and payment options, is listed at www.portugaltolls.com.

Train

Trains (www.cp.pt) run along the coast between Faro and Vila Real de Santo António, and Faro and Lagos (and Loulé). Express trains run to/from the region's main towns to Lisbon.

Essential Information

Accessible Travel

- The Algarve is better than the rest of Portugal accessibility-wise, but awareness is nonetheless limited. Public offices and agencies are required to provide access and facilities for people with disabilities.
- Faro Airport has accessible toilets.
- Dedicated parking spaces are widely available. The EU parking card entitles visitors to the same street-parking concessions given to disabled residents. Newer and larger hotels tend to have adapted rooms, though the facilities may not be up to scratch; ask detailed questions before booking.
- Most camping grounds have accessible toilets and some hostels have disabled facilities.

Business Hours

Things tend to shut down for an hour or two around lunchtime, so do as the locals do and sit down for a meal.

Banks 8.30am to 3pm Monday to Friday

Bars 7pm to 2am
Cafes 9am to 7pm

Clubs 11pm to 4am Thursday to Saturday
Restaurants Noon to 3pm and 7pm to 10pm

Shops 9.30am to noon and 2pm to 7pm Monday to Friday, 10am to 1pm Saturday

Electricity

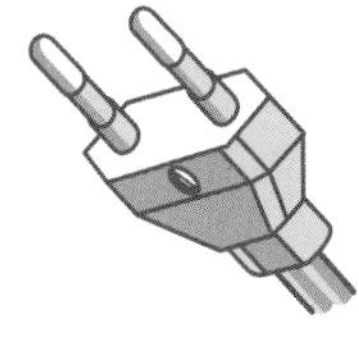

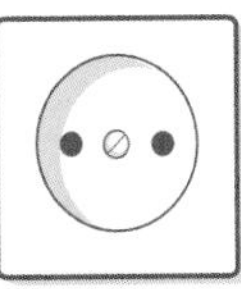

Type C
220V/50Hz

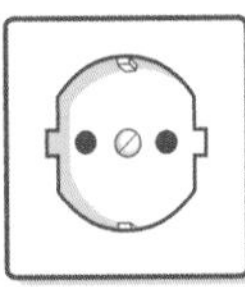

Type F
230V/50Hz

Emergency

Dial ☎112 for any emergency.

Money

Credit cards are accepted by most accommodation operators and upper-end restaurants.

ATMs

ATMs are widespread. Check to see what your home bank will charge you for withdrawals.

Cash

Portugal uses the euro (€). There are notes of 5, 10, 20, 50, 100, 200 and 500 euros, and coins of 1, 2, 5, 10, 20 and 50 cents, and €1 and €2.

Changing Money

There are plenty of exchange offices and banks to change cash.

Tipping

Bars Not expected unless table service is provided, then around 10%.

Hotels One euro per bag is standard; gratuity for cleaning staff is at your discretion.

Restaurants On average 10%, up to 15% in pricier places.

Snack bars It's courteous to leave a bit of spare change.

Taxis Not expected, but it's polite to round up to the nearest euro.

Public Holidays

New Year's Day
1 January

Carnaval Tuesday
Tuesday before Ash Wednesday (February/March)

Good Friday
March/April

Easter Monday
March/April

Money-Saving Tips

- At lunchtime, restaurants often serve a *prato do dia* (daily special), usually great value at around €8 to €12.
- The Passe Turístico (Tourist Pass; www.eva-bus.com) gives you unlimited travel on Eva and Frota Azul buses for three (€30.40) or seven (€38) days.
- If you're near the Spanish border, nip across to fill up with petrol; it's invariably cheaper.

Liberty Day 25 April (celebrating the 1974 revolution)

Labour Day 1 May

Corpus Christi 60 days after Easter Sunday

Portugal Day 10 June (also known as Camões and Communities Day)

Feast of the Assumption 15 August

Republic Day 5 October

All Saints' Day 1 November

Restoration of Independence Day 1 December

Feast of the Immaculate Conception 8 December

Christmas Day 25 December

Safe Travel

- Petty theft is prevalent. *Never* leave valuables unattended in the car or on the beach.
- Especially on the west coast, beware of dangerous ocean currents and strong winds. Check beaches' coloured flags: chequered means the beach is unsupervised, red means it's currently unsafe, yellow means paddle but don't swim, and green means it's safe to swim. Blue means the beach is safe and clean.
- Cliff instability is a problem, especially heading westwards from Lagos. Erosion is ongoing and serious rock falls and smaller landslides can occur. Heed the signs at the beaches and along the cliffs.

Telephone

Codes & Calls To call Portugal from abroad, dial the international access code (☎00), then Portugal's country code (☎351), then the number. All domestic numbers have nine digits, and there are no area codes.

Roaming International roaming charges have been abolished within the EU for EU phones.

SIMs The main domestic operators are Vodafone, Optimus and TMN. All sell prepaid SIM cards that you can insert into a GSM mobile phone and use as long as the phone is not locked by your service provider.

Toilets

- Most towns and villages that draw tourists have free public toilets.
- The *mercado municipal* (municipal market) often has free toilets. These are generally fairly clean and adequately maintained.
- In more built-up areas, your best bet is to look for a toilet in a shopping centre or duck into a cafe (ask first!).

Tourist Information

- The Algarve's tourist website (www.visitalgarve.pt) is excellent; download brochures, maps and various publications.
- Locally managed *postos de turismo* (tourist offices; usually signposted *turismo*) offer good multilingual map brochures and varying degrees of help.
- Turismo de Portugal, the country's national tourist board, also operates an informative website: www.visitportugal.com.
- Useful Algarve tourist offices:

Aljezur (282 998 229; www.visitalgarve.pt; Rua 25 de Abril 62; 9.30am-1pm & 2-7pm daily Jul & Aug, 9.30am-1pm & 2-5.30pm Tue-Sat Sep-Jun)

Faro (www.visitalgarve.pt; Rua da Misericórdia 8; 9.30am-1pm & 2-5.30pm;)

Lagos (282 763 031; www.visitalgarve.pt; Praça Gil Eanes 17; 9.30am-1pm & 2-5.30pm)

Loulé (289 463 900; www.visitalgarve.pt; Avenida 25 de Abril 9; 9.30am-1pm & 2-5.30pm Mon-Fri)

Monchique (282 911 189; www.visitalgarve.pt; Largo de São Sebastião; 9.30am-1pm & 2-5.30pm Mon-Fri)

Sagres (282 624 873; www.visitalgarve.pt; Rua Comandante Matoso 75; 9.30am-1pm & 2-7pm daily Jul & Aug, 9.30am-1pm & 2-5.30pm Tue-Sat Sep-Jun)

Silves (282 098 927; www.visitalgarve.pt; Parque Ribeirinho de Silves; 9.30am-1pm & 2-5.30pm Tue-Sat)

Tavira (281 322 511; www.visitalgarve.pt; Praça da República 5; 9am-1pm & 2-5pm)

Couvert

At restaurants, waiters bring bread, olives etc to your table when you sit down. This unordered appetiser is called the *couvert* and it is never free (prices vary depending on the establishment). If you don't want it, send it away and check it isn't accidentally added to your bill.

Visas

- Until 2021, citizens of Australia, Canada, Japan, New Zealand and the USA don't need visas for tourist visits for stays of up to 90 days.
- From 2021, non-EU nationals who don't require a visa for entry to the Schengen area will need prior authorisation to enter under the new European Travel Information and Authorisation System (ETIAS; www.etias.com). Travellers can apply online; the cost will be €7 for a three-year, multi-entry authorisation.
- Nationals of other countries (eg South Africa) will need a Schengen visa.

Language

Most sounds in Portuguese are also found in English. The exceptions are the nasal vowels (represented in our pronunciation guides by '*ng*' after the vowel), pronounced as if you're trying to make the sound through your nose; and the strongly rolled *r* (represented by '*rr*' in our pronunciation guides). Also note that the symbol '*zh*' sounds like the 's' in 'pleasure'. Keeping these few points in mind and reading the pronunciation guides as if they were English, you'll be understood just fine. The stressed syllables are indicated with italics.

To enhance your trip with a phrasebook, visit lonelyplanet.com. Lonely Planet iPhone phrasebooks are available through the Apple App store.

Basics

Hello. *Olá.* o·*laa*

Goodbye. *Adeus.* a·de·*oosh*

How are you?
Como está? ko·moo shtaa

Fine, and you?
Bem, e você? beng e vo·se

Please.
Por favor. poor fa·vor

Thank you.
Obrigado. (m) o·bree·gaa·doo
Obrigada. (f) o·bree·gaa·da

Excuse me.
Faz favor. faash fa·vor

Sorry. *Desculpe.* desh·kool·pe

Yes./No. *Sim./Não.* seeng/nowng

I don't understand.
Não entendo. nowng eng·teng·doo

Do you speak English?
Fala inglês? faa·la eeng·glesh

Eating & Drinking

..., please. *..., por favor.* ... poor fa·vor

A coffee *Um café* oong ka·fe

A table for two *Uma mesa para duas pessoas* oo·ma me·za pa·ra doo·ash pe·so·ash

Two beers *Dois cervejas* doysh ser·ve·zhash

I'm a vegetarian.
Eu sou vegetariano/vegetariana. (m/f)
e·oo soh ve·zhe·a·ree·a·noo/ ve·zhe·a·ree·a·na

Cheers!
Saúde! sa·oo·de

That was delicious!
Isto estava delicioso!
eesh·too shtaa·va de·lee·see·o·zoo

The bill, please.
A conta, por favor.
a kong·ta poor fa·vor

Shopping

I'd like to buy ...
Queria comprar ... ke·ree·a kong·praar ...

I'm just looking.
Estou só a ver. shtoh so a ver

How much is it?
Quanto custa? *kwang·too koosh·ta*

It's too expensive.
Está muito caro.
shtaa mweeng·too kaa·roo

Can you lower the price?
Pode baixar o preço?
po·de bai·shaar oo pre·soo

Emergencies

Help!
Socorro! *soo·ko·rroo*

Call a doctor!
Chame um médico! *shaa·me oong me·dee·koo*

Call the police!
Chame a polícia!
shaa·me a poo·lee·sya

I'm sick.
Estou doente. *shtoh doo·eng·te*

I'm lost.
Estou perdido. (m) *shtoh per·dee·doo*
Estou perdida. (f) *shtoh per·dee·da*

Where's the toilet?
Onde é a casa de banho?
ong·de e a kaa·za de ba·nyoo

Time & Numbers

What time is it?
Que horas são? *kee o·rash sowng*

It's (10) o'clock.
São (dez) horas. *sowng (desh) o·rash*

Half past (10).
(Dez) e meia. *(desh) e may·a*

morning	*manhã*	*ma·nyang*
afternoon	*tarde*	*taar·de*
evening	*noite*	*noy·te*
yesterday	*ontem*	*ong·teng*
today	*hoje*	*o·zhe*
tomorrow	*amanhã*	*aa·ma·nyang*
1	*um*	*oong*
2	*dois*	*doysh*
3	*três*	*tresh*
4	*quatro*	*kwaa·troo*
5	*cinco*	*seeng·koo*
6	*seis*	*saysh*
7	*sete*	*se·te*
8	*oito*	*oy·too*
9	*nove*	*no·ve*
10	*dez*	*desh*

Transport & Directions

Where's ...?
Onde é ...? *ong·de e ...*

What's the address?
Qual é o endereço?
kwaal e oo eng·de·re·soo

Can you show me (on the map)?
Pode-me mostrar (no mapa)?
po·de·me moosh·traar (noo maa·pa)

When's the next bus?
Quando é que sai o próximo autocarro?
kwang·doo e ke sai oo pro·see·moo ow·to·kaa·rroo

I want to go to ...
Queria ir a ... *ke·ree·a eer a ...*

Does it stop at ...?
Pára em ...? *paa·ra eng ...*

Please stop here.
Por favor pare aqui.
poor fa·vor paa·re a·kee

Behind the Scenes

Send Us Your Feedback

We love to hear from travellers – your comments help make our books better. We read every word, and we guarantee that your feedback goes straight to the authors. Visit **lonelyplanet.com/contact** to submit your updates and suggestions.

Note: We may edit, reproduce and incorporate your comments in Lonely Planet products such as guidebooks, websites and digital products, so let us know if you don't want your comments reproduced or your name acknowledged. For a copy of our privacy policy visit lonelyplanet.com/legal.

Catherine's

Muitíssimo obrigada first and foremost to Julian, and to all of the locals, fellow travellers and tourism professionals throughout the Algarve who provided insights, information and great times. Huge thanks too to Destination Editor Tom Stainer and the Portugal team, and everyone at Lonely Planet. As ever, *merci encore* to my parents, brother, *belle-sœur*, *neveu* and *nièce*.

Acknowledgements

Cover photograph: Faro (p35), Olimpio Fantuz/4Corners Images ©

This Book

This 2nd edition of Lonely Planet's *Pocket Algarve* guidebook was researched and written by Catherine Le Nevez. The previous edition was written by Andy Symington. This guidebook was produced by the following:

Destination Editor Tom Stainer

Senior Product Editors Sandie Kestell, Genna Patterson

Regional Senior Cartographer Anthony Phelan

Product Editor Shona Gray

Book Designer Jessica Rose

Assisting Editors Janet Austin, Katie Connolly, Melanie Dankel, Sarah Reid, Rosie Nicholson, Kellie Langdon, Lorna Parkes, Gabrielle Stefanos

Cover Researcher Naomi Parker

Thanks to Mark Griffiths, Sandra Henriques Gajjar, Rachel Rawling, Kirsten Rawlings, David Tunley

Index

See also separate subindexes for:
Eating p158
Drinking p159
Entertainment p159
Shopping p159

Sights 000
Map Pages **000**

Sights 000
Map Pages **000**

Eating